Certificate in Accounting

Principles of Bookkeeping Controls

Exam Practice Kit

For assessments from September 2024

Third edition 2024

ISBN: 9781 0355 1644 5

Previous ISBN: 9781 0355 0648 4

e-ISBN: 9781 0355 1679 7

British Library Cataloguing-in-Publication Data

A catalogue record for this book is available from the British Library

Published by

BPP Learning Media Ltd

BPP House, Aldine Place

142–144 Uxbridge Road

London W12 8AA

www.learningmedia.bpp.com

Printed in the United Kingdom

Your learning materials, published by BPP Learning Media Ltd, are printed on paper obtained from traceable sustainable sources.

A note about copyright

Contents

Introduction

This is BPP Learning Media's AAT Exam Practice Kit for *Principles of Bookkeeping Controls*. It is part of a suite of ground-breaking resources produced by BPP Learning Media for AAT assessments.

This Exam Practice Kit has been written in conjunction with the BPP Course Book, and has been carefully designed to enable students to practise all of the learning outcomes and assessment criteria for the units that make up *Principles of Bookkeeping Controls*. It is fully up to date as at April 2024 and reflects both the AAT's qualification specification and the practice assessments provided by the AAT.

This Exam Practice Kit contains these key features:

- Tasks corresponding to each chapter of the Course Book. Some tasks are designed for learning purposes, others are of assessment standard
- Further BPP practice assessments

The emphasis in all tasks and assessments is on the practical application of the skills acquired.

VAT

You may find tasks throughout this Exam Practice Kit that need you to calculate or be aware of a rate of VAT. This is stated at 20% in these examples and questions.

Approaching the assessment

When you sit the assessment it is very important that you follow the on screen instructions. This means you need to carefully read the instructions, both on the introduction screens and during specific tasks.

When you access the assessment you should be presented with an introductory screen with information similar to that shown below (taken from the introductory screen from one of the AAT's Q2022 practice assessments for *Principles of Bookkeeping Controls*).

Assessment information:

You have **1 hour and 30 minutes** to complete this sample assessment.

- This assessment contains **8 tasks** and you should attempt to complete **every** task.
- Each task is independent. You will not need to refer to your answer to previous tasks.
- The total number of marks for this assessment is 80.
- Read every task carefully to make sure you understand what is required.
- Where the date is relevant, it is given in the task data.
- Both minus signs and brackets can be used to indicate negative numbers **unless** task instructions state otherwise.
- You must use a full stop to indicate a decimal point. For example, write 100.57 **not** 100,57 or 10057.
- You may use a comma to indicate a number in the thousands, but you don't have to. For example, 10000 and 10,000 are both acceptable.
- Mathematical rounding should be applied where appropriate.

The actual instructions will vary depending on the subject you are studying for. It is very important you read the instructions on the introductory screen and apply them in the assessment. You don't want to lose marks when you know the correct answer just because you have not entered it in the right format.

In general, the rules set out in the AAT practice assessments for the subject you are studying for will apply in the real assessment, but you should carefully read the information on this screen again in the real assessment, just to make sure. This screen may also confirm the VAT rate used if applicable.

A full stop is needed to indicate a decimal point. We would recommend using minus signs to indicate negative numbers and leaving out the comma signs to indicate thousands, as this results in a lower number of keystrokes and less margin for error when working under time pressure. Having said that, you can use whatever is easiest for you as long as you operate within the rules set out for your particular assessment.

You have to show competence throughout the assessment and you should therefore complete all of the tasks. Don't leave questions unanswered.

In some assessments, written or complex tasks may be human marked. In this case you are given a blank space or table to enter your answer into. You are told in the assessments which tasks these are (note: there may be none if all answers are marked by the computer).

If these involve calculations, it is a good idea to decide in advance how you are going to lay out your answers to such tasks by practising answering them on a word document, and certainly you should try all such tasks in this Exam Practice Kit and in the AAT's environment using the practice assessments.

When asked to fill in tables, or gaps, never leave any blank even if you are unsure of the answer. Fill in your best estimate.

Note that for some assessments where there is a lot of scenario information or tables of data provided (eg tax tables), you may need to access these via 'pop-ups'. Instructions will be provided on how you can bring up the necessary data during the assessment.

Finally, take note of any task specific instructions once you are in the assessment. For example you may be asked to enter a date in a certain format or to enter a number to a certain number of decimal places.

Grading

To achieve the qualification and to be awarded a grade, you must pass all the mandatory unit assessments, all optional unit assessments (where applicable) and the synoptic assessment (where applicable).

The AAT Level 2 Foundation Certificate in Accounting will be awarded a grade. This grade will be based on performance across the qualification. Unit assessments are not individually graded. These assessments are given a mark that is used in calculating the overall grade.

How overall grade is determined

You will be awarded an overall qualification grade (Distinction, Merit, and Pass). If you do not achieve the qualification you will not receive a qualification certificate, and the grade will be shown as unclassified.

The marks of each assessment will be converted into a percentage mark and rounded up or down to the nearest whole number. This percentage mark is then weighted according to the weighting of the unit assessment or synoptic assessment within the qualification. The resulting weighted assessment percentages are combined to arrive at a percentage mark for the whole qualification.

Grade definition	Percentage threshold
Distinction	90–100%
Merit	80–89%
Pass	70–79%
Unclassified	0–69% Or failure to pass one or more assessment/s

Resits

Some AAT qualifications such as the AAT Foundation Certificate in Accounting have restrictions in place for how many times you are able to re-sit assessments. Please refer to the AAT website for further details.

You should only be entered for an assessment when you are well prepared and you expect to pass the assessment.

AAT qualifications

The material in this book may support the following AAT qualifications:

AAT Level 2 Certificate in Accounting

AAT Level 2 Certificate in Bookkeeping

AAT Certificate in Accounting at SCQF Level 6

Supplements

From time to time we may need to publish supplementary materials to one of our titles. This can be for a variety of reasons. From a small change in the AAT unit guidance to new legislation coming into effect between editions.

You should check our supplements page regularly for anything that may affect your learning materials. All supplements are available free of charge on our supplements page on our website at:

learningmedia.bpp.com/pages/resources-for-students

Improving material and removing errors

BPP Learning Media do everything possible to ensure the material is accurate and up to date when sending to print. In the event that any errors are found after the print date, they are uploaded to the following website: https://learningmedia.bpp.com/pages/errata

These learning materials are based on the qualification specification released by the AAT in January 2024.

Questions

Chapter 1 – Payment methods

Task 1.1

Given below are four cheques received by Southfield Electrical today, 9 January 20X6.

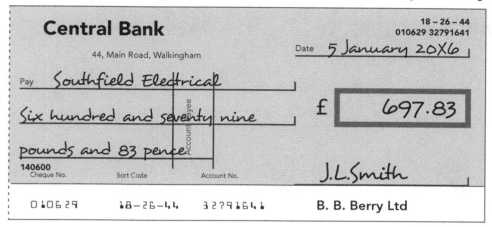

Central Bank

18 – 26 – 44
010629 32791641

44, Main Road, Walkingham

Date 5 January 20X6

Pay Southfield Electrical

Six hundred and seventy nine

pounds and 83 pence

£ 697.83

J.L.Smith

140600
Cheque No.   Sort Code   Account No.

010629   18–26–44   32791641

B. B. Berry Ltd

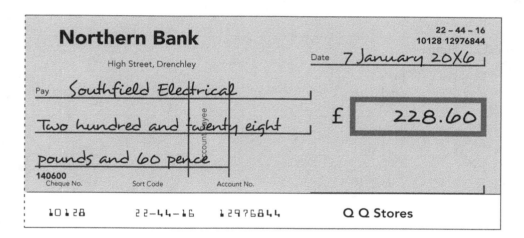

Northern Bank

22 – 44 – 16
10128 12976844

High Street, Drenchley

Date 7 January 20X6

Pay Southfield Electrical

Two hundred and twenty eight

pounds and 60 pence

£ 228.60

140600
Cheque No.   Sort Code   Account No.

10128   22–44–16   12976844

Q Q Stores

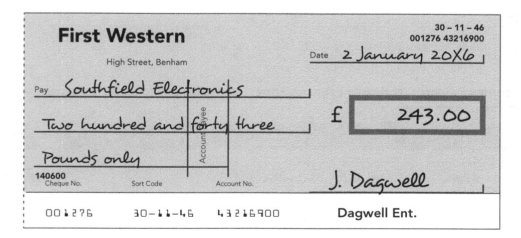

First Western

30 – 11 – 46
001276 43216900

High Street, Benham

Date 2 January 20X6

Pay Southfield Electronics

Two hundred and forty three

Pounds only

£ 243.00

J. Dagwell

140600
Cheque No.   Sort Code   Account No.

001276   30–11–46   43216900

Dagwell Ent.

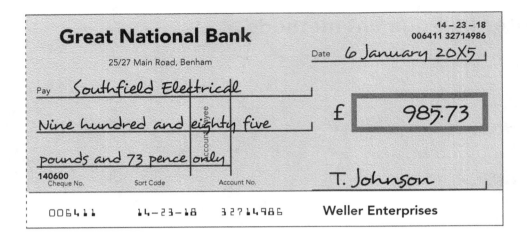

Required

Check each one thoroughly and identify the error on the cheques above, selecting your answer from the picklist.

Comments	
Cheque from B. B. Berry Ltd	▼
Cheque from Q Q Stores	▼
Cheque from Dagwell Enterprises	▼
Cheque from Weller Enterprises	▼

Picklist

- Amount
- Date
- Payee
- Signature

Task 1.2

Frank Limited needs to make several payments to its suppliers.

Required

Select the correct payment method in each case from the picklist provided. You may use the same option more than once.

Situation	Payment method
Payment to Kim Guitars Ltd for £2,500 for items purchased on credit. The payment is required within 5 days.	▼
Payment of £1,000 to Pixie Bass as a deposit on a supply. The payment is required today to release the shipment.	▼
Payment of £265,000 to Paz Ltd to secure a new retail unit. Immediate payment is required.	▼
Payment to Santiago Strings for £875 to pay an invoice due by the end of the week.	▼

Picklist

- BACS direct credit
- CHAPS
- Faster payment

Task 1.3

Complete the following statements by selecting the relevant banking terms from the picklist.

(a) A [▼] would be set up to repay a bank loan in equal monthly instalments.

(b) A [▼] would be set up to make the minimum payment on a credit card by variable amounts each month.

(c) A bank [▼] would be arranged when short-term borrowing is needed.

Picklist

- Direct debit
- Overdraft
- Standing order

Task 1.4

Using the picklist, select the most suitable payment method for each of the business expenses.

Situation	Solution
Making regular rent payments	▼
Purchase of office stationery online	▼
Payment of wages to staff	▼
Payment of £2,500 to a supplier after taking 15 days credit	▼
Buying tea bags for the office	▼
Payment of £375 for new tyres for the company van	▼

Picklist

- BACS direct credit
- Bank draft
- Cash
- Debit card
- Standing order

 BPP

Task 1.5

Which TWO of the following items should be checked when a cheque is accepted as payment from customers?

	✓
Funds are available in customer's account	
Issue number	
Words and figures match	
Security number	
Expiry date	
Date is not in the future	

Task 1.6

The director of Parker Flooring Limited has made a number of payments today (2 February 20X6) in respect of materials for the company.

Required

Select the correct impact on the bank account from the picklist below.

Payment	Impact on the bank account
Cheque written for £550 to Soft Carpets Limited	▼
Debit card to buy diesel for the van £65	▼
Credit card to buy printer cartridges online £30	▼
Payment of a purchase invoice using BACS direct credit to Solvit Limited £1,200	▼
Cheque written for £276 to Wall2Wall Limited	▼
Debit card to buy coffee from the local store of £5.67	▼
Bank draft for £10,000 to purchase a new van	▼

Picklist

- Delayed
- Immediate (within 24 hours)

Task 1.7

Given below is a completed cheque.

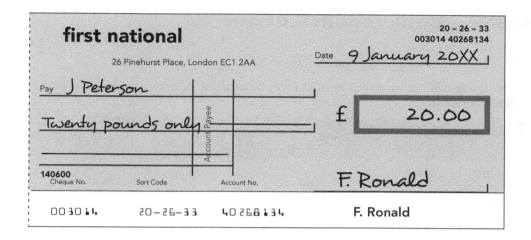

Required

Complete the following statements by selecting from the picklist.

Who is the drawee?	▼
Who is the payee?	▼
Who is the drawer?	▼

Picklist

- F. Ronald
- First National
- J Peterson

Chapter 2 – Bank reconciliations

Task 2.1

Would each of the following transactions appear as a payment in, or a payment out, on a business's bank statement?

Transaction	Payment out ✓	Payment in ✓
£470.47 paid into the bank		
Standing order of £26.79		
Cheque payment of £157.48		
Interest earned on the bank balance		
BACS payment for wages		

Task 2.2

You are given information about Newmans's receipts during the week ending 27 January. They represent payments by credit customers and receipts for sales to non-credit customers of music, instruments and CDs which were settled by cheque.

Details	Type	Amount £
Tunfield DC	Bank transfer	594.69
Tunshire County Orchestra	Bank transfer	468.29
Sale of music	Cheque	478.90
Tunfield Brass Band	Credit	1,059.72
Sale of instruments	Cheque	752.16
Sale of CDs	Cheque	256.80

You need to update the cash book to reflect the impact of these receipts

Required

(a) Enter the correct entries from the picklist provided and total the debit side of the cash book given below.

Cash book - debit side

Date	Details	Bank £
	Bal b/f	379.22
	▼	
	▼	
	▼	
	▼	

Date	Details		Bank
		▼	£
		▼	
	TOTAL		

Picklist

- Non-credit sales
- Tunfield BB
- Tunfield DC
- Tunshire CO

Given below is the credit side of the cash book for Newmans for the week ending 27 January.

Cash book – credit side

Date	Cheque no	Details	Bank
			£
27 Jan	003014	Henson Press	329.00
27 Jan	003015	Ely Instr	736.96
27 Jan	003016	Jester Press	144.67
27 Jan	003017	CD Supplies	74.54
27 Jan	003018	Jester Press	44.79
27 Jan	003019	Buser Ltd	273.48
27 Jan	SO	Rates	255.00
27 Jan	DD	Rent	500.00

Given below is the bank statement for Newmans for the week ending 27 January.

STATEMENT

First National

26 Pinehurst Place

London

EC1 2AA

NEWMANS

CURRENT ACCOUNT

Account number: 40268134

Sheet 023

Date		Paid out	Paid in	Balance
20XX				
20 Jan	Balance b/f			379.22 CR

Date		Paid out	Paid in	Balance
24 Jan	Counter credit – Tunfield		594.69	
	Counter credit – Tunshire Co		468.29	
24 Jan	SO – British Elec	212.00		1,230.20 CR
25 Jan	Counter credit – Tunfield AOS		108.51	1,338.71 CR
26 Jan	Cheque No 003014	329.00		
	Credit		478.90	1,488.61 CR
27 Jan	Cheque No 003017	74.54		
	Cheque No 003015	736.96		
	Credit		1,059.72	
	Credit		752.16	
	SO – TDC	255.00		
	DD – Halpern Properties	500.00		
	Bank interest		3.68	1,737.67 CR

Required

(b) Compare the two sides of the cash book from the information given in part (a) to the bank statement. Note any unmatched items below by selecting items from the picklist below and state whether the item needs including in the cash book or in the bank reconciliation.

Unmatched item		£	Action to be taken	
	▼			▼
	▼			▼
	▼			▼
	▼			▼
	▼			▼
	▼			▼
	▼			▼

Picklist

- Bank charge
- Bank credit
- Bank interest received
- Cheque number 003016
- Cheque number 003018
- Cheque number 003019
- Include on bank reconciliation
- Sales of CDs
- Standing order British Elec
- Update cash book

(c) Using the information available from parts (a) and (b) earlier in this task, consider the required amendments to both sides of the cash book using the picklist provided and enter the balance on the cash book as at 27 January.

Cash book

Date	Details	Bank £	Cheque number	Details	Bank £
	Balance b/f	379.22	003014	Henson Press	329.00
27 Jan	Tunfield DC	594.69	003015	Ely Instr	736.96
27 Jan	Tunshire CO	468.29	003016	Jester Press	144.67
27 Jan	Non-credit sales	478.90	003017	CD Supplies	74.54
27 Jan	Tunfield BB	1,059.72	003018	Jester Press	44.79
27 Jan	Non-credit sales	752.16	003019	Buser Ltd	273.48
27 Jan	Non-credit sales	256.80	SO	Rates	255.00
27 Jan	▼		DD	Rent	500.00
27 Jan	▼			▼	
				▼	
	Total			Total	

Picklist

- Balance b/f
- Balance c/d
- Bank charges
- Bank interest
- Standing order
- Tunfield AOS
- Tunfield DC

(d) Identify the FOUR reconciling items below to prepare the bank reconciliation statement as at 27 January.

Bank reconciliation statement	£
Balance as per bank statement	
Add:	
▼	
▼	
Total to add	
Less:	
▼	
▼	

Bank reconciliation statement		£
▼		
Total to subtract		
Balance as per cash book		

Picklist

- Cheque 003014
- Cheque 003015
- Cheque 003016
- Cheque 003017
- Cheque 003018
- Cheque 003019
- Credit sales
- DD
- Non-credit sales
- SO

Task 2.3

On 28 November, The Flower Chain received the following bank statement.

High Street Bank plc				
The Concourse, Badley, B72 5DG				
To: The Flower Chain Account no: 28710191 **Date:** 25 November				
Statement of Account				

Date	Details	Paid out £	Paid in £	Balance £
03 Nov	Balance b/f			9,136 C
07 Nov	Cheque 110870	6,250		2,886 C
17 Nov	Cheque 110872	2,250		636 C
21 Nov	Cheque 110865	3,670		3,034 D
	Direct Debit – Insurance Ensured	500		3,534 D
21 Nov	Counter Credit – BBT Ltd		10,000	6,466 C
24 Nov	Counter credit – Petals Ltd		2,555	9,021 C
	Direct Debit – Rainbow Ltd	88		8,933 C
25 Nov	Cheque 110871	1,164		7,769 C
D = Debit C = Credit				

The cash book, as at 28 November, is shown after the requirements.

Required

(i) Match the items on the bank statement against the items in the cash book.

(ii) Update the cash book as needed using the picklist and entering the cheque or reference details, plus the amount.

(iii) Total the cash book and clearly show the balance carried down at 28 November AND brought down at 29 November.

(iv) Using the picklist provided, identify the FOUR transactions that are included in the cash book but missing from the bank statement and complete the bank reconciliation statement as at 28 November.

Cash book

Date	Details	Bank £	Date	Cheque number	Details	Bank £
01 Nov	Balance b/f	5,466	03 Nov	110870	Roberts & Co	6,250
24 Nov	Bevan & Co	1,822	03 Nov	110871	J Jones	1,164
24 Nov	Plant Pots Ltd	7,998	06 Nov	110872	Lake Walks Ltd	2,250
	(1) ▼		10 Nov	110873	PH Supplies	275
	(1) ▼		17 Nov	110874	Peters & Co	76
					(1) ▼	
					(1) ▼	
					(1) ▼	
	Total				Total	
	(1) ▼					

Bank reconciliation statement as at 28 November		£
Balance as per bank statement		
Add:		
(2)	▼	
(2)	▼	
Total to add		
Less:		
(2)	▼	
(2)	▼	
Total to subtract		
Balance as per cash book		

Picklist 1

- BBT Ltd

- Balance b/d
- Balance c/d
- Insurance Ensured
- Petals Ltd
- Peters & Co
- Rainbow Ltd

Picklist 2
- Bevan & Co
- PH Supplies
- Peters & Co
- Plant Pots Ltd

Task 2.4

(a) **Which TWO of the following items reconciling the cash book to the bank statement are referred to as timing differences? Tick the appropriate box in the table below.**

	✓
Bank charges not recorded in the cash book	
Outstanding lodgements	
Interest charged not recorded in the cash book	
Unpresented cheques	

Your cash book at 31 December shows a bank balance of £565 overdrawn. On comparing this with your bank statement at the same date, you discover the following:

- A cheque for £57 drawn by you on 29 December has not yet been presented for payment.
- A cheque for £92 from a customer, which was paid into the bank on 24 December, has been dishonoured on 31 December.

Required

(b) **The correct cash book balance at 31 December is:**

	✓
£714 overdrawn	
£657 overdrawn	
£473 overdrawn	
£530 overdrawn	

The cash book shows a bank balance of £5,675 overdrawn at 31 August. It is subsequently discovered that a standing order for £125 has been entered in the cash book twice, and that a dishonoured cheque for £450 has been debited in the cash book instead of credited.

Required

(c) Select the correct bank balance:

	✓
£5,100 overdrawn	
£6,000 overdrawn	
£6,250 overdrawn	
£6,450 overdrawn	

Task 2.5

Your firm's cash book at 30 April shows a balance at the bank of £2,490. Comparison with the bank statement at the same date reveals the following differences:

Transactions	Amount
	£
Unpresented cheques	840
Bank charges	50
Receipts not yet credited by the bank	470
Dishonoured cheque from customer	140

Required

(a) Select the correct balance on the cash book at 30 April:

	✓
£1,460	
£2,300	
£2,580	
£3,140	

The bank statement at 31 December 20X1 shows a balance of £1,000. The cash book shows a balance of £750.

Required

(b) Which of the following is the most likely reason for the difference?

	✓
Receipts of £250 recorded in the cash book, but not yet recorded by bank	
Bank charges of £250 shown on the bank statement, not in the cash book	
Standing orders of £250 included on bank statement, not in the cash book	
Cheques issued for £250 recorded in the cash book, but not yet gone through the bank account	

Your firm's cash book at 30 April shows a balance at the bank of £3,526. Comparison with the bank statement at the same date reveals the following differences:

 BPP

	£
Unpresented cheques	920
Bank interest received not in cash book	150
Uncredited lodgements	270
Dishonoured customer's cheque	310

Required

(c) **The correct cash book balance at 30 April is:**

£ [   ]

Task 2.6

On 26 July, Ottaways Ltd received the following bank statement from Ronda Bank, as at 23 July. Assume today's date is 28 July.

	Ronda Bank PLC			
	Bank Buildings, Flitweck, FT87 1XQ			
To: Ottaways Ltd	Account No 56235472		23 July	
	Bank Statement			

Date 20XX	Detail	Paid out £	Paid in £	Balance £	
03 Jul	Balance b/f			1,855	C
03 Jul	Cheque 126459	3,283		1,428	D
03 Jul	Cheque 126460	1,209		2,637	D
03 Jul	Cheque 126461	4,221		6,858	D
04 Jul	Cheque 126464	658		7,516	D
09 Jul	Counter credit SnipSnap Co		8,845	1,329	C
11 Jul	Cheque 126462	1,117		212	C
11 Jul	Direct Debit Flit DC	500		288	D

Date 20XX	Detail	Paid out £	Paid in £	Balance £	
18 Jul	Direct Debit Consol Landlords	475		763	D
20 Jul	Bank Charges	32		795	D
22 Jul	Interest for month	103		898	D
23 Jul	Counter credit		5,483	4,585	C

Date	Detail		Paid out £	Paid in £	Balance £
20XX					
		D = Debit C = Credit			

The cash book as at 23 July is shown after the requirements.

Required

(i)   Match the items on the bank statement against the items in the cash book.

(ii) Using the picklist below for the details column, enter any items in the cash book as needed.

(iii) Total the cash book and clearly show the balance carried down at 23 July and brought down at 24 July.

(iv) Using the picklist below, complete the bank reconciliation statement as at 23 July.

Date	Details		Bank £	Date	Cheque number	Details	Bank £
01 Jul	Balance b/f		1,855	01 Jul	126459	Gumpley Co	3,283
20 Jul	Brimfull Ltd		5,483	01 Jul	126460	Warnes Ltd	1,209
21 Jul	Adera Ltd		2,198	01 Jul	126461	Veldt Partners	4,221
22 Jul	Mist Northern		1,004	01 Jul	126462	Pathways	1,117
		▼		02 Jul	126463	Lindstrom Co	846
				02 Jul	126464	Kestrels Training	658
				13 Jul	126465	HGW Ltd	3,200
				13 Jul		Flit DC	500
						▼	
						▼	
						▼	
						▼	
	Total					Total	
		▼					

Bank reconciliation statement as at 23 July	£
Balance per bank statement	
Add:	
▼	
▼	
Total to add	
Less:	
▼	

Bank reconciliation statement as at 23 July		£
▼		
Total to subtract		
Balance as per cash book		

Picklist

- Adera Ltd
- Balance b/d
- Balance c/d
- Bank charges
- Brimfull Ltd
- Consol Landlords
- Flit DC
- Gumpley Co
- HGW Ltd
- Interest
- Kestrels Training
- Lindstrom Co
- Mist Northern
- Pathways
- SnipSnap Co
- Veldt Partners
- Warnes Ltd

BPP

Chapter 3 – Introduction to control accounts

Task 3.1

Assuming they all INCLUDE VAT where relevant, identify the double entry for the following transactions.

Here is a list of the transactions for August 20XX

	£
Credit purchases	3,390
Credit sales returns	1,860
Payments to credit suppliers	4,590
Receipts from credit customers	5,480
Discounts allowed	400
Discounts received	200

Required

Show the journal entries needed to record the following:

(a) Purchases

Account		Amount £	Debit	Credit
	▼			
	▼			
	▼			

(b) Sales returns

Account		Amount £	Debit	Credit
	▼			
	▼			
	▼			

(c) Payments to credit suppliers

Account		Amount £	Credit	Credit
	▼			
	▼			

 BPP

(d) Receipts from credit customers

Account	Amount £	Debit	Credit
▼			
▼			

Picklist

- Bank
- Discounts allowed
- Discounts received
- Payables ledger control
- Purchases
- Receivables ledger control
- Sales returns
- VAT control

Task 3.2

Your organisation is not registered for VAT. The balance on the receivables ledger control account on 1 January was £11,689. The transactions that took place during January are summarised below:

Transaction	Amount £
Credit sales	12,758
Sales returns	1,582
Cash received from trade receivables	11,563
Discounts allowed	738

Required

You are required to write up the receivables ledger control account using the picklist below for the month of January.

Receivables ledger control

Details	Amount £	Details	Amount £
▼		▼	
▼		▼	
		▼	
		▼	

Picklist

- Balance b/f
- Balance c/d
- Bank
- Discounts allowed
- Sales
- Sales returns

Task 3.3

Your organisation is not registered for VAT. The opening balance on the payables ledger control account at 1 January was £8,347. The transactions for the month of January have been summarised below:

Transactions	Amount £
Credit purchases	9,203
Purchases returns	728
Payments to trade payables	8,837
Discounts received	382

Required

You are required to write up the payables ledger control account for the month of January.

Payables ledger control

Details	Amount £	Details	Amount £
▼		Balance b/f	
▼		▼	
▼			
▼			

Picklist

- Balance c/d
- Bank
- Discounts received
- Purchases
- Purchases returns

Task 3.4

This is a summary of transactions with credit suppliers during June.

Transactions	Amounts £
Balance of trade payables at 1 June	85,299
Goods bought on credit – gross	39,300
Payments made to credit suppliers	33,106
Discounts received	1,000
Goods returned to credit suppliers – gross	275

Required

Prepare a payables ledger control account from the details shown in the table on the prior page. Show clearly the balance carried down at 30 June AND brought down at 1 July.

Payables ledger control account

Date	Details	Amount £	Date	Details	Amount £
	▼			Balance b/f	
	▼			▼	
	▼				
	▼				
				▼	

Picklist

- Balance b/d
- Balance c/d
- Bank
- Discounts received
- Purchases
- Purchases returns

Task 3.5

The receivables ledger control account at 1 May had a balance of £31,475. During May, gross sales of £125,000 were made on credit. Receipts from trade receivables amounted to £122,500 and discounts of £550 were allowed. Credit notes of £1,300 gross were issued to customers.

Required

(a) The closing balance on the receivables ledger control account at 31 May is:

	✓
£32,125	
£33,975	
£34,725	
£33,225	

Your payables ledger control account has a balance at 1 October of £34,500 credit. During October, gross credit purchases were £78,400, gross cash purchases were £2,400 and payments made to suppliers, excluding cash purchases, and after deducting settlement discounts of £1,200, were £68,900. Gross purchases returns were £4,700.

Required

(b) The closing balance on the payables ledger control account was:

	✓
£38,100	
£40,500	
£47,500	
£49,900	

Task 3.6

Sunshine Limited has calculated its VAT for the month of March. It has a VAT control account credit balance of £4,500 brought down on 1 March 20XX.

There are a number of transactions made during the month.

Details	Amount
	£
VAT on sales	6,000
VAT on sales returns	300
VAT on purchases	2,500
Bank payment made to HMRC	7,000
VAT on purchases returns	250

Required

(a) Prepare the VAT control account for March 20XX. Show the balance c/d at 31 March 20XX and the balance b/d at 1 April 20XX.

Details	Amount	Details	Amount
	£		**£**
▼		Balance b/f	4,500

BPP

Details	Amount £	Details	Amount £
▼		▼	
▼		▼	
▼			
		▼	

Picklist

- Balance b/d
- Balance c/d
- Payment to HMRC
- VAT on purchase returns
- VAT on purchases
- VAT on sales
- VAT on sales returns

(b) **If VAT of £4,500 was calculated on sales made by Sunshine Limited during April 20XX, and there were no other VAT transactions, what would be the liability to HMRC at 30 April 20XX?**

£ _____

Chapter 4 – Preparing and reconciling control accounts

Task 4.1

When reconciling receivables ledger and payables ledger control accounts to the list of balances from the subsidiary ledgers, would the following errors affect the relevant control account, the list of balances or both?

	Control account ✓	List of balances ✓	Both ✓
Invoice entered into the sales daybook as £980 instead of £890			
Purchases daybook overcast by £1,000			
Discounts allowed of £20 not entered into the cash book (debit side)			
An invoice taken as £340 instead of £440 when being posted to the customer's account			
Incorrect balancing of a memorandum ledger account			
A purchases return not entered into the purchases returns daybook			

Task 4.2

James has just completed his first month of trading. James makes sales on credit to four customers and the transactions during his second month of trading were as follows. James is not registered for VAT.

Transactions	Amount £
Sales to H Simms	2,000
Sales to P Good	2,700
Sales to K Mitchell	1,100
Sales to C Brown	3,800
Receipt from H Simms	2,400
Receipts from P Good	3,600
Receipts from K Mitchell	1,100
Receipts from C Brown	4,800

Required

You are required to:

 BPP

(i) Using the picklist, show these transactions in total in the receivables ledger control account and in detail in the individual receivables ledger accounts. Each of the accounts shows, where appropriate, the opening balance at the start of the second month.

(ii) Balance the receivables ledger control account and the individual receivables ledger accounts.

(iii) Reconcile the list of receivables ledger balances to the balance on the control account.

Receivables ledger control account

Details	Amount £	Details	Amount £
Balance b/f	5,000	▼	
▼		▼	
▼			

Receivables ledger

H Simms

Details	Amount £	Details	Amount £
Balance b/f	900	▼	
▼		▼	
▼		▼	

P Good

Details	Amount £	Details	Amount £
Balance b/f	1,600	▼	
▼		▼	
▼			

K Mitchell

Details	Amount £	Details	Amount £
▼		▼	

C Brown

Details	Amount		Details		Amount
	£				£
Balance b/f	2,500			▼	
		▼		▼	
		▼			

Reconciliation of receivables ledger balances with the control account balance

	£
H Simms	
P Good	
K Mitchell	
C Brown	
Receivables ledger control account	

Picklist

- Balance b/d
- Balance c/d
- Bank
- Sales

Task 4.3

James also buys goods on credit from three suppliers. The transactions with these suppliers in month two are summarised below. James is not registered for VAT.

Transactions	Amount
	£
Purchase from J Peters	1,600
Purchase from T Sands	2,500
Purchase from L Farmer	3,200

Transactions	Amount
	£
Payment to J Peters	1,700
Payment to T Sands	3,200
Payment to L Farmer	3,000

Required

You are required to:

(1) Using the picklist, show these transactions in total in the payables ledger control account and in detail in the individual payables ledger accounts. Each of the accounts shows, where appropriate, the opening balance at the start of the second month.

(2) Balance the payables ledger control account and the individual payables ledger accounts.

(3) Reconcile the list of payables ledger balances to the balance on the control account.

Payables ledger control

Details	Amount £	Details	Amount £
▼		Balance b/f	2,700
▼		▼	
		▼	

Payables ledger

J Peters

Details	Amount £	Details	Amount £
▼		Balance b/f	300
▼		▼	
		▼	

T Sands

Details	Amount £	Details	Amount £
▼		Balance b/f	1,700
▼		▼	
		▼	

L Farmer

Details	Amount £	Details	Amount £
▼		Balance b/f	700

Details	Amount £	Details	Amount £
▼		▼	
		▼	

Reconciliation of payables ledger balances with control account balance

	£
J Peters	
T Sands	
L Farmer	
Payables ledger control account	

Picklist
- Balance b/d
- Balance c/d
- Bank
- Purchases

Task 4.4

The following are the receivables ledger transactions for June 20XX

Transactions	Amount £
Items sold on credit	14,500
Returns from customers	700
Receipts from customers	15,600

Required

(a) **You are required to write up the receivables ledger control account. Please use the picklist provided:**

Receivables ledger control

Details	Amount £	Details	Amount £
Balance b/f	9,450	▼	
▼		▼	
		▼	

 BPP

Details	Amount £	Details	Amount £
▼			

Picklist

- Balance b/d
- Balance c/d
- Bank
- Returns
- Sales on credit

The following are the balances on the receivables ledger.

Details	Amount £
Annabel Limited	3,000
Bahira Limited	1,250
Clara Limited	3,310

Required

(b) What is the difference between the receivables ledger control account and the receivables ledger?

£ [   ]

(c) Which TWO of the following reasons could explain why there is this difference between the receivables ledger control account and the receivables ledger?

	✓
A cash receipt was incorrectly entered onto the customer's account in the receivables ledger	
A sales invoice has been duplicated in the receivables ledger	
A sales return credit note has only been recorded in the receivables ledger control account	
Discounts have been posted twice in the customer's receivables ledger account	

Task 4.5

The following is an extract of the balances on the payables ledger as at 31 July 20XX.

Transactions	Amount £
Goods purchased on credit during July	8,600
Payments made to credit suppliers in July	9,750

Transactions	Amount
	£
Discounts received	500

The brought forward balance at 1 July 20XX was £12,500.

Required

(a) Complete the payables ledger control account using the balances above. Remember to calculate the balance brought down at 1 August 20XX.

Payables ledger control

Details	Amount	Details	Amount
	£		£
▼		Balance b/f	
▼		▼	
▼			
		▼	

Picklist

- Balance b/d
- Balance c/d
- Bank
- Discounts received
- Purchases

The following are the balances on the payables ledger as at 31 July 20XX:

Payables ledger

Transactions	Amount
	£
Cargo Transport Limited	5,400
Utilities Financing Limited	1,200
Airborne Parcels Limited	2,000
LoGist Limited	1,250
Wrap Around Limited	800

Required

(b) Using the information from the payables ledger in part (a), complete the payables ledger account reconciliation in the table below.

	£
Payables ledger control account balance as at 31 July 20XX	

 BPP

	£
Total of the payables ledger accounts as at 31 July 20XX	
Difference	

(c) **Select the ONE correct possible reason for this difference on the payables ledger reconciliation.**

	✓
Purchases on credit have been recorded on the debit side of the payables ledger	
A purchase invoice has been duplicated in the payables ledger	
Discounts received have been omitted from the payables ledger but recorded in the payables ledger control account	
A cash payment to a credit supplier has been booked to the payables ledger control account only	

Task 4.6

This is a summary of your business's transactions with credit customers during November.

	£
Balance of trade receivables at 1 November	48,125
Goods sold on credit (gross value)	37,008
Money received from credit customers	28,327
Discounts allowed	240
Goods returned by customers (gross value)	2,316

Required

(a) **Using the picklist provided below, prepare a receivables ledger control account from the details shown above. Show clearly the balance carried down at 30 November AND brought down at 1 December.**

Receivables ledger control

Date	Details	Amount £	Date	Details		Amount £
	Balance b/f				▼	
	▼				▼	
					▼	
					▼	
	▼					

Picklist

- Balance b/d
- Balance c/d
- Bank
- Discounts allowed
- Sales
- Sales returns

The following balances were in the receivables ledger on 1 December:

Transactions	Amount £
J Hicks Ltd	3,298
Parks and Gardens	4,109
Greener Grass	18,250
TTL Ltd	18,106
Reeves and Wright	10,400

Required

(b) Reconcile the balances shown above with the receivables ledger control account balance you have calculated in part (a).

	£
Receivables ledger control account balance as at 1 December	
Total of receivables ledger accounts as at 1 December	
Difference	

(c) Because of an error in the receivables ledger, there is a difference. What might have caused the difference? Tick TWO reasons only.

	✓
VAT has been overstated on an invoice.	
VAT has been understated on an invoice.	
A sales invoice has been entered in the receivables ledger twice.	
A sales credit note has been entered in the receivables ledger twice.	
A receipt from a customer has been omitted from the receivables ledger.	
A receipt from a customer has been entered in the receivables ledger twice.	

Task 4.7

The following transactions take place during a three month period (the entity's first trading period)

Required

(a) Calculate the VAT on the balances and complete the table below (round your answers to the nearest pound).

 BPP

Transactions	Amount £	VAT £
Sales on credit including VAT at 20%	106,800	
Purchases on credit including VAT at 20%	54,000	
Credit notes issued including VAT at 20%	2,820	

(b) Using the VAT figures calculated above, complete the VAT control account, including the balance brought down at the end of the quarter. Use the picklist provided.

VAT control

Details	Amount £	Details	Amount £
▼		▼	
▼			
▼			
		▼	

Picklist

- Balance b/d
- Balance c/d
- Purchases
- Sales
- Sales returns

(c) The amount payable to HMRC for the quarter will be

£ [   ]

Task 4.8

At the end of the last VAT period, the VAT account for Fast Fashions showed that a refund was due from HM Revenue & Customs.

Required

(a) Select ONE reason that would cause a refund to be due to Fast Fashions.

	✓
The receivables ledger control account shows a difference to the receivables ledger account balances	
Sales were less than purchases for the quarter	
There was an underpayment of VAT in the previous quarter	

Sales in June totalled £129,240, all including VAT.

Required

(b) What is the amount of output VAT on sales?

£ [   ]

Task 4.9

A supplier sends you a statement showing a balance outstanding of £14,350. Your own records show a balance outstanding of £14,500.

Required

(a) The reason for this difference could be that

	✓
The supplier sent an invoice for £150 which you have not yet received	
The supplier has given you £150 settlement discount which you had not entered in your ledger	
You have paid the supplier £150 which he has not yet accounted for	
You have returned goods worth £150 which the supplier has not yet accounted for	

An invoice for £69 has been recorded in the sales daybook as £96.

Required

(b) When the receivables ledger reconciliation is prepared, adjustments will be required to:

	✓
The control account only	
The list of balances only	
Both the control account and the list of balances	

At the end of the month, the payables ledger control account has credit entries amounting to £76,961 and debit balances amounting to £24,500.

The following transactions need to be recorded in the payables ledger control account:

- Correction of a duplicated supplier's invoice for £4,688
- Standing order payments to suppliers of £1,606

Required

(c) What will be the corrected payables ledger control account balance brought down after the transactions above have been recorded? Tick the correct entry to show whether this balance will be a debit or a credit.

Amount	Debit	Credit
£	✓	✓

Task 4.10

You have been handed an aged receivable analysis which shows a total balance of £109,456.

Required

(a) This amount should reconcile with which TWO of the following?

	✓
The balance on the bank statement	
The balance on the receivables ledger control account	
The balance on the payables ledger control account	
The total of all the payables ledger balances	
The total of all the receivables ledger balances	

(b) Complete the following sentence:

The aged receivable analysis shows:

	✓
How much is owed to suppliers at any point	
Over how many months the outstanding balance owed by each individual credit customer has built up	
The total purchases over the year to date to each credit supplier	

Task 4.11

A credit customer, B B Brand Ltd, has ceased trading, owing Kitchen Kuts £1,560 plus VAT.

Required

(a) Record the journal entries needed in the general ledger to write off the net amount and the VAT.

Account name	Amount £	Debit ✓	Credit ✓
▼			
▼			
▼			

Picklist

- Irrecoverable debts
- Receivables ledger control
- VAT control

Kitchen Kuts has the following transactions for the month (all figures include VAT):

- Credit sales of £8,400
- Purchases of £540
- Sales returns of £300

Required

(b) Record the transactions above in the VAT control account, including the entries for the irrecoverable debt of B B Brand Ltd and the VAT brought down figure for the following month. Use the picklist provided.

VAT control account

Details	Amount £	Details	Amount £
		Balance b/f	250
▼		▼	
▼			
▼			
▼			
		▼	

Picklist

- Balance b/d
- Balance c/d
- Irrecoverable debt expense
- Purchases
- Sales
- Sales returns

Task 4.12

A credit customer, ABC Ltd, has ceased trading, owing your firm £240 plus VAT.

Required

Prepare a journal to write off the net amount and VAT in the general ledger.

Journal

Account name	Amount £	Debit ✓	Credit ✓
▼			
▼			
▼			

Picklist

- Irrecoverable debt expense
- Receivables ledger control
- VAT control

 BPP

Task 4.13

Textile Carpets has a credit customer, Flooring King, who has ceased trading, owing the business £2,370. Textile Carpets is registered for VAT at 20%

Required

Record the journal entries needed in the general ledger to write off the net amount and the VAT.

Account name		Amount £	Debit ✓	Credit ✓
	▼			
	▼			
	▼			

Picklist

- Irrecoverable debt expense
- Receivables ledger control
- VAT control

Chapter 5 – The journal

Task 5.1

An organisation has started a new business and a new set of accounts is to be opened. The opening balances for the new business are as follows:

Details	Amount £
Capital	10,000
Furniture and fittings	15,315
Motor vehicles	20,109
Cash at bank	15,000
Payables ledger control	37,238
Receivables ledger control	12,524
Loan from bank	7,000
VAT (owed to HM Revenue & Customs)	8,710

Required

Using the picklist below, prepare a journal to enter these opening balances into the accounts.

Journal

Account name	Debit £	Credit £
▼		
▼		
▼		
▼		
▼		
▼		
▼		
▼		
Totals		

Picklist

- Capital
- Cash at bank
- Furniture and fittings
- Loan from bank
- Motor vehicles
- Payables ledger control

- Receivables ledger control
- VAT (owed to HM Revenue & Customs)

Task 5.2

A new business has already started to trade, though it is not yet registered for VAT, and now wishes to open up its first set of accounts. You are handed the following information:

	£
Bank	300
Petty cash	200
Trade receivables	7,700
Bank loan	9,000
VAT	1,300
Trade payables	3,400
Van	6,000
Capital	500

Required

Record the journal entries needed in the accounts in the general ledger of the business to deal with the opening entries. Use the picklist below to select your account, write in the amount to be entered and tick the appropriate entry to show whether a debit or a credit.

Account name	Amount £	Debit ✓	Credit ✓
▼			
▼			
▼			
▼			
▼			
▼			
▼			
▼			

Picklist

- Bank
- Capital
- Loan from bank
- Petty cash
- Trade payables
- Trade receivables
- VAT control (owed to HM Revenue & Customs)

- Van

Task 5.3

Kitchen Kuts has started a new business, Kitchen Capers, and a new set of accounts is to be opened. A partially completed journal to record the opening entries is shown below.

Required

Record the journal entries needed in the accounts in the general ledger of Kitchen Capers to deal with the opening entries.

Account name	Amount £	Debit ✓	Credit ✓
Cash	150		
Cash at bank	12,350		
Capital	23,456		
Fixtures and fittings	2,100		
Trade receivables	3,206		
Loan from bank	10,000		
Motor vehicle	15,650		

Task 5.4

Peter Knight is one of the employees at Short Furniture. The payroll department have calculated his payroll for May as follows.

Details	Amount £
Gross wages	2,200
National Insurance Contributions (Employee)	183
National Insurance Contributions (Employer)	200
Income Tax	256

Required

(a) **Calculate Peter's net wages for the month.**

£ [   ]

(b) **Show how all of the elements of Peter's wages including the net wages as shown in part (a) would be entered into the accounting records by using the picklist below and writing up the ledger accounts given.**

Wages expense

Details	Amount £	Details	Amount £
▼			
▼			

Wages control

Details	Amount £	Details	Amount £
▼		▼	
▼		▼	
▼			
▼			

HMRC control

Details	Amount £	Details	Amount £
		▼	
		▼	
		▼	

Bank

Details	Amount £	Details	Amount £
		▼	

Picklist

- Bank
- HMRC control
- Wages control
- Wages expense

Task 5.5

Select the correct recipient of each of the following payroll related costs.

	Employee ✓	HMRC ✓	Pension company ✓	Employer ✓
Income Tax				

	Employee ✓	HMRC ✓	Pension company ✓	Employer ✓
NIC (employee)				
Pension contributions				
Net wages				

Task 5.6

Georgia Blossom has her monthly wages paid to her on the 28th of the month. She pays into the pension scheme and her employer contributes an additional 4% of her gross wages as pension contributions.

These are the calculations for Georgia's August 20XX wages.

	Amount £
Gross wages	3,500
Pension contribution by Georgia	200
Income Tax	500
NIC (employee)	180
NIC (employer)	210
Trade union subscription	15

Required

(a) Calculate the employer's pension contribution

£ [   ]

(b) Calculate Georgia's net wages for August

£ [   ]

(c) Transfer the pension liability from the wages control account to the pension liability account, using the picklist below.

Journal

Details	Debit £	Credit £
▼		
▼		

Picklist

- Pension administrator
- Wages control

(d) Complete the journal for the trade union subscription deduction.

 BPP

Journal

Details		Debit £	Credit £
	▼		
	▼		

Picklist

- Trade union subscription
- Wages control

(e) Complete the journal for the payment of the net wages to Georgia on the 28th.

Details		Debit £	Credit £
	▼		
	▼		

Picklist

- Bank
- Wages control

(f) What is the total monthly cost to the company of employing Georgia?

£ [   ]

Task 5.7

Jamila employs 10 people in her business. At 31 March, she needs to prepare a journal to reflect the following information:

- Gross pay to employees – £14,168
- Income tax deducted from gross pay – £823
- National insurance contributions deducted from gross pay – £781
- Employers national insurance contributions – £240

Required

Complete the journal entries below by entering the correct amount in either the debit or credit column for each line.

Date	Nominal Code	Debit £	Credit £
31 March	8000 – Gross wages		
31 March	8004 – Employer NI		
31 March	1220 – PAYE		
31 March	1221 – National Insurance		
31 March	1220 – Net wages		

Chapter 6 – Initial trial balance

Task 6.1

You are given the following account balances from the general ledger of your organisation.

Required

Would each balance be a debit or a credit balance in the trial balance?

Ledger account	Balance	Debit ✓	Credit ✓
Sales	592,513		
Telephone	1,295		
Receivables ledger control	52,375		
Wages	104,288		
Purchases returns	8,229		
Bank overdraft	17,339		
Purchases	372,589		
Drawings	71,604		
Sales returns	32,800		
Car	14,700		
Payables ledger control	31,570		

Task 6.2

Below are two general ledger accounts and a partially completed trial balance at 31 January 20XX.

Office equipment

Date 20XX	Details	Amount £	Date 20XX	Details	Amount £
9 Jan	Balance b/f	29,502	1 Jan	Journal	350
31 Jan	Bank	7,288	21 Jan	Balance c/d	36,440
		36,790			36,790

Purchases

Date 20XX	Details	Amount £	Date 20XX	Details	Amount £
1 Jan	Balance b/f	89,920	30 Jan	Balance c/d	196,800
30 Jan	Payables ledger control	106,880			

Date 20XX	Details	Amount £	Date 20XX	Details	Amount £
		196,800			196,800

Required

Complete the trial balance by:

- Transferring the balances of the two general ledger accounts to the debit or credit column of the trial balance;
- Entering the amounts shown against each of the other account names into the debit or credit column of the trial balance; and
- Totalling both columns of the trial balance.

Do not enter figures with decimal places in this task and do not enter a zero in unused column cells.

	£	Debit £	Credit £
Office equipment			
Purchases			
Motor vehicles	76,800		
Sales	285,600		
Bank (overdraft)	2,016		
Petty cash	36		
Capital	90,000		
Sales returns	5,640		
Purchases returns	4,320		
Receivables ledger control	42,960		
Payables ledger control	36,120		
VAT (owed to HMRC)	15,540		
Drawings	12,040		
Telephone	1,920		
Electricity	3,360		
Wages	74,520		
Loan from bank	36,000		
Discounts allowed	7,680		
Discounts received	4,680		
Rent expense	16,080		
Totals			

Task 6.3

The double-entry system of bookkeeping normally results in which of the following balances on the ledger accounts? Tick ONE.

Debit balances	Credit balances	✓
Assets and income	Liabilities, capital and expenses	
Income, capital and liabilities	Assets and expenses	
Assets and expenses	Liabilities, capital and income	
Assets, expenses and capital	Liabilities and income	

Task 6.4

What does a credit balance on a ledger account indicate? Tick ONE.

	✓
An asset or an expense	
A liability or an expense	
An amount owing to the organisation	
A liability or income	

Task 6.5

Which of the following balances would be a credit balance on a trial balance?

	✓
Non-current assets	
Sales returns	
Discounts allowed	
Bank overdraft	

Task 6.6

Given below is the list of ledger balances for your organisation at 31 August.

Required

You are required to prepare a trial balance as at 31 August.

	£	Debit £	Credit £
Bank (overdraft)	4,838		
Capital	216,000		
Discounts allowed	18,432		
Discounts received	11,232		

 BPP

	£	Debit £	Credit £
Drawings	28,896		
Electricity	8,064		
Loan from bank	86,400		
Motor vehicles	184,320		
Office equipment	87,456		
Petty cash	100		
Purchases	472,320		
Payables ledger control	86,688		
Purchases returns	10,368		
Rent expense	38,592		
Sales	685,440		
Receivables ledger control	103,104		
Sales returns	13,536		
Telephone	4,608		
VAT (owed to HMRC)	37,310		
Wages	178,848		
Totals			

Chapter 7 – Errors and the trial balance

Task 7.1

A suspense account has been opened with a balance of £180.

The error has been identified as an entry made in the general ledger from the incorrectly totalled net column in the sales daybook shown below.

Sales daybook

Date 20XX	Details		Invoice number	Total	VAT	Net
				£	£	£
29 Sep	F Bacon		2349	768	128	640
30 Sep	J Locke		2350	1,476	246	1,230
30 Sep	D Hume		2351	2,040	340	1,700
	Totals			4,284	714	3,750

Required

(a) Record the journal entries needed to:

- Remove the incorrect entry
- Record the correct entry
- Remove the suspense account balance

Do not enter a zero in unused debit or credit column cells.

Journal to remove the incorrect entry

Account name		Debit	Credit
		£	£
▼			

Journal to record the correct entry

Account name		Debit	Credit
		£	£
▼			

Journal to remove the suspense account balance

Account name		Debit	Credit
		£	£
▼			

Picklist

- Receivables ledger control
- Sales

- Sales returns
- Suspense
- VAT control

Another error has been found in the general ledger. Entries to record cash drawings of £350 has been reversed.

Required

(b) Record the journal entries needed to:
- **Remove the incorrect entries**
- **Record the correct entries**

Do not enter a zero in unused debit or credit column cells.

Journal to remove the incorrect entries

Account name		Debit £	Credit £
	▼		
	▼		

Journal to record the correct entries

Account name		Debit £	Credit £
	▼		
	▼		

Picklist
- Bank
- Capital
- Cash
- Drawings

Task 7.2

A business extracts a trial balance in which the debit column totals £452,409 and the credit column totals £463,490.

Required

What will be the balance on the suspense account? Tick whether this balance will be a debit or a credit.

Account name	Amount	Debit ✓	Credit ✓
Suspense			

Task 7.3

A business used a suspense account with a credit balance of £124 to balance its initial trial balance.

Required

Correction of which ONE of the following errors will clear the suspense account?

	✓
A credit note from a supplier with a net amount of £124 was not entered in the payables ledger	
Discounts allowed of £124 were only posted to the discounts allowed account	
A cash purchase for £124 was not entered in the purchases account	
An irrecoverable debt write-off of £124 was not entered in the subsidiary ledger	

Task 7.4

A suspense account has been opened with a balance of £54.

The error has been identified as an entry made in the general ledger from the incorrectly totalled VAT column in the purchases daybook shown below.

Purchases daybook

Date	Details	Invoice number	Total	VAT	Net
20XX			£	£	£
31 Dec	I Kant	5521	1,002	167	835
31 Dec	G Hegel	5522	264	44	220
31 Dec	K Marx	5523	1,902	317	1,585
	Totals		3,168	582	2,640

Required

(a) Record the journal entries needed to:

- Remove the incorrect entry
- Record the correct entry
- Remove the suspense account balance

Do not enter a zero in unused debit or credit column cells.

Journal to remove the incorrect entry

Account name	Debit	Credit
	£	£
▼		

Journal to record the correct entry

Account name		Debit £	Credit £
▼			

Journal to remove the suspense account balance

Account name		Debit £	Credit £
▼			

Picklist

- Payables ledger control
- Purchases
- Suspense
- VAT control

Another error has been found in the general ledger. Entries to record cash purchases of £800 have been reversed. (Ignore VAT.)

Required

(b) Record the journal entries needed to:

- **Remove the incorrect entries**
- **Record the correct entries**

Do not enter a zero in unused debit or credit column cells.

Journal to remove the incorrect entries

Account name		Debit £	Credit £
▼			
▼			

Journal to record the correct entries

Account name		Debit £	Credit £
▼			
▼			

Picklist

- Bank
- Capital
- Cash
- Purchases

Task 7.5

A suspense account has been opened with a balance of £270.

The error has been identified as an entry made in the general ledger from the incorrectly totalled net column in the sales returns daybook shown below.

Date	Details	Invoice number	Total	VAT	Net
20XX			£	£	£
31 Dec	Klein	4839	1,944	324	1,620
31 Dec	Bion	4840	546	91	455
31 Dec	Winnicott	4841	5,604	934	4,670
	Totals		8,094	1,349	6,475

Required

(a) Record the journal entries needed to:

- Remove the incorrect entry
- Record the correct entry
- Remove the suspense account balance

Do not enter a zero in unused debit or credit column cells.

Journal to remove the incorrect entry

Account name		Debit	Credit
		£	£
▼			

Journal to record the correct entry

Account name		Debit	Credit
		£	£
▼			

Journal to remove the suspense account balance

Account name		Debit	Credit
		£	£
▼			

Picklist

- Bion
- Klein
- Receivables ledger control
- Sales returns
- Suspense
- VAT control

- Winnicott

Another error has been found in the general ledger. An entry to record a bank receipt from a credit customer settled by counter credit of £450 has been reversed.

Required

(b) Record the journal entries needed to:

- **Remove the incorrect entries**
- **Record the correct entries**

Do not enter a zero in unused debit or credit column cells.

Journal to remove the incorrect entries

Account name		Debit £	Credit £
	▼		
	▼		

Journal to record the correct entries

Account name		Debit £	Credit £
	▼		
	▼		

Picklist

- Bank
- Payables ledger control
- Purchases
- Receivables ledger control
- Sales
- Suspense
- VAT

Task 7.6

After extracting an initial trial balance a business finds it has a debit balance of £118 in the suspense account. A number of errors have been noted.

Required

(a) **Using the picklists below, record the journal entries needed in the general ledger to reverse the incorrect entries and record the transactions correctly.**

Sales of £500 have been credited to the sales returns account.

Details		Debit £	Credit £
	▼		

Details	Debit £	Credit £
▼		

(b) Entries to record a bank payment of £125 for office expenses have been reversed.

Details	Debit £	Credit £
▼		
▼		
▼		
▼		

(c) A bank payment of £299 for purchases (no VAT) has been entered correctly in the purchases column of the cash book but as £29 in the total column.

Details	Debit £	Credit £
▼		
▼		
▼		
▼		
▼		

(d) Discounts allowed of £388 were only posted to the receivables ledger control account in the general ledger.

Details	Debit £	Credit £
▼		
▼		

Details	Debit £	Credit £
▼		
▼		

Picklist

- Discounts allowed
- Receivables ledger control
- Suspense

Task 7.7

On 30 June, a suspense account of a business that is not registered for VAT has a credit balance of £720.

On 1 July, the following errors were discovered:

(1) A bank payment of £225 has been omitted from the rent and rates account.

(2) An irrecoverable debt expense of £945 has been credited correctly to the receivables ledger control account, but debited to both the irrecoverable debt account and the sales account.

Required

(i) Enter the opening balance in the suspense account below.

(ii) Make the necessary entries to clear the suspense account using the picklist below.

Suspense

Date	Details	Amount £	Date	Details	Amount £
	▼			▼	
	▼			▼	

Picklist

- Balance b/f
- Rent and rates
- Sales

Task 7.8

When posting an invoice received for building maintenance, £980 was entered on the building maintenance expense account instead of the correct amount of £890. In each case, select the correct option from the table below.

Required

(a) What correction should be made to the building maintenance expenses account?

Debit £90	
Credit £90	
Debit £1,780	
Credit £1,780	

A business receives an invoice from a supplier for £2,800 which is mislaid before any entry has been made, resulting in the transaction being omitted from the books entirely.

Required

(b) This is an

Error of transposition	
Error of omission	
Error of principle	
Error of commission	

(c) An error of commission is one where

A transaction has not been recorded	
One side of a transaction has been recorded in the wrong account, and that account is of a different class to the correct account	
One side of a transaction has been recorded in the wrong account, and that account is of the same class as the correct account	
A transaction has been recorded using the wrong amount	

(d) Which ONE of the following is an error of principle?

A gas bill credited to the gas account and debited to the bank account	
The purchase of a non-current asset credited to the asset account and debited to the supplier's account	
The purchase of a non-current asset debited to the purchases account and credited to the supplier's account	
The payment of wages debited and credited to the correct accounts, but using the wrong amount	

Task 7.9

(a) Where a transaction is entered into the correct ledger accounts, but the wrong amount is used, the error is known as an error of

	✓
Omission	
Original entry	
Commission	
Principle	

When a trial balance was prepared, two ledger accounts were omitted:

Discounts received   £6,150

Discounts allowed   £7,500

A suspense account was opened.

Required

(b) What was the balance on the suspense account?

	✓
Debit £1,350	
Credit £1,350	
Debit £13,650	
Credit £13,650	

(c) If a purchases return of £48 has been wrongly posted to the debit of the sales returns account, but has been correctly entered in the payables ledger control account, the total of the trial balance would show

	✓
The credit side to be £48 more than the debit side	
The debit side to be £48 more than the credit side	
The credit side to be £96 more than the debit side	
The debit side to be £96 more than the credit side	

(d) Indicate whether preparing a trial balance will reveal the following errors.

	Yes ✓	No ✓
Omitting both entries for a transaction		
Posting the debit entry for an invoice to an incorrect expense account		
Omitting the debit entry for a transaction		
Posting the debit entry for a transaction as a credit entry		

 BPP

Task 7.10

Show which of the errors below are, or are not, disclosed by the trial balance.

Error in the general ledger	Error disclosed by the trial balance ✓	Error NOT disclosed by the trial balance ✓
Recording a bank receipt of a cash sale on the debit side of the cash sales account		
Entering an insurance expense in the administration expenses account		
Entering the discounts received account balance on the debit side of the trial balance		
Miscasting the total column of one page of the sales returns daybook		
Failing to write up a dishonoured cheque in the cash book		
Recording discount allowed of £15 as £150 in the cash book		

Task 7.11

Your organisation's trial balance included a suspense account. All the bookkeeping errors have now been traced and the journal entries shown below have been recorded.

Journal entries

Account name	Debit £	Credit £
Motor vehicles	4,300	
Machinery		4,300
Suspense	750	
Receivables ledger control		750
Discounts allowed	209	
Suspense		209

Required

Post the journal entries to the general ledger accounts. Dates are not required but you must complete the 'details' columns accurately.

Discounts allowed

Details	Amount £	Details	Amount
▼		▼	

Machinery

Details	Amount	Details	Amount
▼		▼	

Motor vehicles

Details	Amount £	Details	Amount £
▼		▼	

Receivables ledger control

Details	Amount £	Details	Amount £
▼		▼	

Suspense

Details	Amount £	Details	Amount £
▼		Balance b/f	541
▼		▼	

Picklist

- Discounts allowed
- Machinery
- Motor vehicles
- Receivables ledger control
- Suspense

Task 7.12

Your business extracted an initial trial balance which did not balance, and a suspense account with a debit balance of £6,290 was opened. Journal entries were subsequently prepared to correct the errors that had been found, and clear the suspense account. The list of balances in the initial trial balance, and the journal entries to correct the errors, are shown below.

Journal entries

Account name	Debit £	Credit £
Receivables ledger control account	2,875	
Suspense		2,875
Receivables ledger control account	2,875	
Suspense		2,875

Account name	Debit £	Credit £
Heat and light		5,172
Suspense	5,172	
Heat and light	5,712	
Suspense		5,712

Required

Taking into account the journal entries, which will clear the suspense account, redraft the trial balance by writing the figures in the debit or credit column.

	Balances extracted on 30 June £	Balances at 1 July	
		Debit £	Credit £
Machinery	82,885		
Computer equipment	41,640		
Insurance	17,520		
Bank (overdraft)	13,252		
Petty cash	240		
Receivables ledger control	241,500		
Payables ledger control	134,686		
VAT (owing to HM Revenue and Customs)	19,920		
Capital	44,826		
Sales	525,092		
Purchases	269,400		
Purchases returns	16,272		
Wages	61,680		

 BPP

	Balances extracted on 30 June	Balances at 1 July Debit	Balances at 1 July Credit
	£	£	£
Maintenance expenses	3,283		
Stationery	8,049		
Rent and rates	3,466		
Heat and light	5,172		
Telephone	7,596		
Marketing expenses	5,327		
	Totals		

Task 7.13

Kitchen Kuts' initial trial balance includes a suspense account with a balance of £100.

The error has been traced to the sales returns daybook shown below.

Sales returns daybook

Date 20XX	Details	Credit note number	Total	VAT	Net
			£	£	£
30 June	Barber Bates Ltd	367	720	120	600
30 June	GTK Ltd	368	4,320	720	3,600
30 June	Peer Prints	369	960	160	800
	Totals		6,000	1,100	5,000

Required

(a) Identify the error and record the journal entries needed in the general ledger to

(i) Remove the incorrect entry

Account name	Amount	Debit	Credit
	£	✓	✓
▼			

(ii) Record the correct entry

Account name	Amount	Debit	Credit
	£	✓	✓
▼			

 BPP

(iii) **Remove the suspense account balance**

Account name		Amount £	Debit ✓	Credit ✓
▼				

An entry to record a bank payment of £350 for heat and light has been reversed.

Required

(b) **Record the journal entries needed in the general ledger to**

(i) **Remove the incorrect entries**

Account name		Amount £	Debit ✓	Credit ✓
▼				
▼				

(ii) **Record the correct entries**

Account name		Amount £	Debit ✓	Credit ✓
▼				
▼				

Picklist

- Bank
- Heat and light
- Suspense
- VAT

Answers

Chapter 1 – Payment methods

Task 1.1

	Comments
Cheque from B. B. Berry Ltd	Amount
Cheque from Q Q Stores	Signature
Cheque from Dagwell Enterprises	Payee
Cheque from Weller Enterprises	Date

Explanations

	Comments
Cheque from B. B. Berry Ltd	Amount: Words and figures differ – they should match to verify the correct amount payable.
Cheque from Q Q Stores	Signature: Cheque is unsigned. Cheques must be signed by an authorised signatory.
Cheque from Dagwell Enterprises	Payee: Payee name is incorrect – Electronics instead of Electrical.
Cheque from Weller Enterprises	Date: Dated 6 January 20X5 instead of 20X6 – this cheque is therefore out of date. Although cheques have no expiry date, generally accepted banking convention says that cheques are not accepted after six months. This is due to the possibility of duplication of payment or this being a stolen cheque.

Task 1.2

Situation	Payment method
Payment to Kim Guitars Ltd for £2,500 for items purchased on credit. The payment is required within 5 days.	BACS direct credit
Payment of £1,000 to Pixie Bass as a deposit on a supply. The payment is required today to release the shipment.	Faster payment
Payment of £265,000 to Paz Ltd to secure a new retail unit. Immediate payment is required.	CHAPS
Payment to Santiago Strings for £875 to pay an invoice due by the end of the week.	BACS direct credit

Explanations

	Payment method	Comment
Payment to Kim Guitars Ltd for £2500 for items purchased on credit. The payment is required within five days.	BACS direct credit	No urgency on the payment, so BACS is sufficient

 BPP

	Payment method	Comment
Payment of £1000 to Pixie Bass as a deposit on a supply. The payment is required today to release the shipment.	Faster payment	Same day money transfer is required
Payment of £265,000 to Paz Ltd to secure a new retail unit. Immediate payment is required.	CHAPS	A highly secure way of moving large amounts of money
Payment to Santiago Strings for £875 to pay an invoice due by the end of the week.	BACS direct credit	No urgency on the payment, so BACS direct credit is sufficient

Task 1.3

(a) A standing order would be set up to repay a bank loan in equal monthly instalments.

(b) A direct debit would be set up to make the minimum payment on a credit card by variable amounts each month.

(c) A bank overdraft would be arranged when short-term borrowing is needed.

Task 1.4

Situation	Solution
Making regular rent payments	Standing order
Purchase of office stationery online	Debit card
Payment of wages to staff	BACS direct credit
Payment of £2,500 to a supplier after taking 15 days credit	BACS direct credit
Buying tea bags for the office	Cash
Payment of £375 for new tyres for the company van	Debit card

A standing order will ensure that regular, same value payments are made on the same day every month to ensure the rent is paid on time without fail.

Buying office stationery online requires payment by a debit (or credit) card.

Payment of wages by BACS direct credit ensures that the money is securely sent to the correct recipient. It also reduces the amount of cash which is kept on the business premises.

Payments to supplier after receipt of an invoice are made by BACS. This ensures the correct amount is sent directly to the correct recipient, within the credit terms set. Payment may also be made by cheque, but this is not an option in this scenario.

Teabags and small items for the office are usually purchased using petty cash, due to the small payments required.

The tyres would have required immediate payment at the garage, so the debit card would be the most suitable form of payment as it securely ensures immediate payment.

Task 1.5

The correct answers are:

	✓
Funds are available in customer's account	
Issue number	
Words and figures match	✓
Security number	
Expiry date	
Date is not in the future	✓

Task 1.6

Payment	Impact on the bank account
Cheque written for £550 to Soft Carpets Limited	Delayed
Debit card to buy diesel for the van £65	Immediate (within 24 hours)
Credit card to buy printer cartridges online £30	Delayed
Payment of a purchase invoice using BACS direct credit to Solvit Limited £1,200	Immediate (within 24 hours)
Cheque written for £276 to Wall2Wall Limited	Delayed
Debit card to buy coffee from the local store of £5.67	Immediate (within 24 hours)
Bank draft for £10,000 to purchase a new van	Immediate (within 24 hours)

Explanations

Payment	Impact on the bank account	Comment
Cheque written for £550 to Soft Carpets Limited	Delayed	The money leaves Parker Flooring's account when the cheque is presented at the bank which may be several days after the cheque was issued
Debit card to buy diesel for the van £65	Immediate	Usually reflected in the bank account within a few hours as the debit card draws money from the account
Credit card to buy printer cartridges online £30	Delayed	This will be charged to the credit card account, and the only impact on the bank will be once the monthly payment to the credit card company is made, therefore a delayed impact

 BPP

ANSWERS

Payment	Impact on the bank account	Comment
Payment of a purchase invoice using BACS Direct Credit to Solvit Limited £1200	Immediate	Parker Flooring will see the cash leave their account immediately, although it may take up to three days to be shown in the supplier account. It depends on the banks
Cheque written for £276 to Wall2Wall Limited	Delayed	The money leaves Parker Flooring's account when the cheque is presented at the bank which may be several days
Debit card to buy coffee from the local store of £5.67	Immediate	Usually reflected in the bank account within a few hours as the debit card draws money from the account
Bank draft for £10,000 to purchase a new van	Immediate	Although the bank draft cheque is drawn on the bank's current account, the bank will immediately withdraw the funds from Parker Flooring's account once they authorise the draft

Task 1.7

Who is the drawee?	First National
Who is the payee?	J Peterson
Who is the drawer?	F. Ronald

Chapter 2 – Bank reconciliations

Task 2.1

The correct answers are:

Transaction	Payment out ✓	Payment in ✓
£470.47 paid into the bank		✓
Standing order of £26.79	✓	
Cheque payment of £157.48	✓	
Interest earned on the bank balance		✓
BACS payment for wages	✓	

Task 2.2

(a)

Cash book - debit side

Date	Details	Bank £
	Bal b/f	379.22
27 Jan	Tunfield DC	594.69
27 Jan	Tunshire CO	468.29
27 Jan	Non-credit sales	478.90
27 Jan	Tunfield BB	1,059.72
27 Jan	Non-credit sales	752.16
27 Jan	Non-credit sales	256.80
	TOTAL	3,989.78

(b)

Unmatched item	£	Action to be taken
Bank credit	108.51	Update cash book
Standing order British Elec	212.00	Update cash book
Bank interest received	3.68	Update cash book
Sales of CDs	256.80	Include on bank reconciliation
Cheque number 003016	144.67	Include on bank reconciliation
Cheque number 003018	44.79	Include on bank reconciliation
Cheque number 003019	273.48	Include on bank reconciliation

Explanations

Unmatched item	£	Action to be taken	Explanation
Bank credit	108.51	Update cash book	This must be checked to any supporting documentation such as any remittance advice from Tunfield AOS or the original invoice – when it has been checked the amount should be entered into the cash book
Standing order British Elec	212.00	Update cash book	The standing order schedule should be checked to ensure that this is correct and it should then be entered into the cash book
Bank interest received	3.68	Update cash book	This should be entered into the cash book
Sales of CDs	256.80	Include on bank reconciliation	The £256.80 cash sales of CDs settled by cheque do not appear on the bank statement. This is an outstanding lodgement that will appear in the bank reconciliation statement
Cheque number 003016	144.67	Include on bank reconciliation	Unpresented cheque – will appear in the bank reconciliation statement
Cheque number 003018	44.79	Include on bank reconciliation	Unpresented cheque – will appear in the bank reconciliation statement
Cheque number 003019	273.48	Include on bank reconciliation	Unpresented cheque – will appear in the bank reconciliation statement

(c)

Cash book

Date	Details	Bank £	Cheque number	Details	Bank £
	Balance b/f	379.22	003014	Henson Press	329.00
27 Jan	Tunfield DC	594.69	003015	Ely Instr	736.96
27 Jan	Tunshire CO	468.29	003016	Jester Press	144.67
27 Jan	Non-credit sales	478.90	003017	CD Supplies	74.54
27 Jan	Tunfield BB	1,059.72	003018	Jester Press	44.79
27 Jan	Non-credit sales	752.16	003019	Buser Ltd	273.48
27 Jan	Non-credit sales	256.80	SO	Rates	255.00
27 Jan	Bank interest	3.68	DD	Rent	500.00

Date	Details		Bank £	Cheque number	Details	Bank £
27 Jan	Tunfield AOS		108.51	SO	Standing order British Elec	212.00
					Balance c/d	1,531.53
	Total		4,101.97		Total	4,101.97

(d)

Bank reconciliation statement	£
Balance as per bank statement	1,737.67
Add:	
Non-credit sales	256.80
Total to add	256.80
Less:	
Cheque 003016	144.67
Cheque 003018	44.79
Cheque 003019	273.48
Total to subtract	462.94
Balance as per cash book	1,531.53

Task 2.3

Cash book

Date	Details	Bank £	Date	Cheque number	Details	Bank £
01 Nov	Balance b/f	5,466	03 Nov	110870	Roberts & Co	6,250
24 Nov	Bevan & Co	1,822	03 Nov	110871	J Jones	1,164
24 Nov	Plant Pots Ltd	7,998	06 Nov	110872	Lake Walks Ltd	2,250
21 Nov	BBT Ltd	10,000	10 Nov	110873	PH Supplies	275
24 Nov	Petals Ltd	2,555	17 Nov	110874	Peters & Co	76
			21 Nov	DD	Insurance Ensured	500
			24 Nov	DD	Rainbow Ltd	88
			28 Nov		Balance c/d	17,238
	Total	27,841			Total	27,841

ANSWERS

Date	Details	Bank £	Date	Cheque number	Details	Bank £
29 Nov	Balance b/d	17,238				

Cheque number 110865 on the bank statement: the first cheque in the cash book in November is number 110870. As the difference between the opening balances on the bank statement and in the cash book is for the amount of this cheque (£3,670) it is reasonable to assume that cheque 110865 was entered in the cash book in a previous month and would have been a reconciling item in the bank reconciliation in the previous month. This cheque should be ticked to the October bank reconciliation.

Bank reconciliation statement as at 28 November	£
Balance as per bank statement	7,769
Add:	
Bevan & Co	1,822
Plant Pots Ltd	7,998
Total to add	9,820
Less:	
PH Supplies	275
Peters & Co	76
Total to subtract	351
Balance as per cash book	17,238

Task 2.4

(a) The correct answers are:

	✓
Bank charges not recorded in the cash book	
Outstanding lodgements	✓
Interest charged not recorded in the cash book	
Unpresented cheques	✓

(b) The correct answer is:

	✓
£714 overdrawn	
£657 overdrawn	✓
£473 overdrawn	
£530 overdrawn	

Working

£(565) o/d – £92 dishonoured cheque = £(657) o/d.

The £57 will not yet have affected the bank account as not been presented at bank yet, hence it does not affect the bank balance as at 31 December.

(c) The correct answer is:

	✓
£5,100 overdrawn	
£6,000 overdrawn	
£6,250 overdrawn	
£6,450 overdrawn	✓

Working

	£	£
Balance b/f		5,675
Reversal – Standing order entered twice	125	
Reversal – Dishonoured cheque entered in error as a debit		450
Correction – Dishonoured cheque		450
Balance c/d (overdraft)	6,450	
	6,575	6,575

Task 2.5

(a) The correct answer is:

	✓
£1,460	
£2,300	✓
£2,580	
£3,140	

Working

	£
Cash book balance	2,490
Adjustment re charges	(50)
Adjustment re dishonoured cheque from customer	(140)
	2,300

 BPP

(b) The correct answer is:

	✓
Receipts of £250 recorded in the cash book, but not yet recorded by bank	
Bank charges of £250 shown on the bank statement, not in the cash book	
Standing orders of £250 included on bank statement, not in the cash book	
Cheques issued for £250 recorded in the cash book, but not yet gone through the bank account	✓

All the other options would give the bank account £250 less than the cash book.

(c) £ 3,366

Working

	£
Balance per cash book	3,526
Plus: bank interest received	150
Less: dishonoured cheque	(310)
Amended cash book balance	3,366

Task 2.6

Date	Details	Bank £	Date	Cheque number	Details	Bank £
01 Jul	Balance b/f	1,855	01 Jul	126459	Gumpley Co	3,283
20 Jul	Brimfull Ltd	5,483	01 Jul	126460	Warnes Ltd	1,209
21 Jul	Adera Ltd	2,198	01 Jul	126461	Veldt Partners	4,221
22 Jul	Mist Northern	1,004	01 Jul	126462	Pathways	1,117
9 Jul	SnipSnap Co	8,845	02 Jul	126463	Lindstrom Co	846
			02 Jul	126464	Kestrels Training	658
			13 Jul	126465	HGW Ltd	3,200
			13 Jul		Flit DC	500
			18 Jul		Consol Landlords	475
			20 Jul		Bank charges	32
			22 Jul		Interest	103
			23 Jul		Balance c/d	3,741
	Total	19,385			Total	19,385
24 Jul	Balance b/d	3,741				

 BPP

Bank reconciliation statement as at 23 July	£
Balance per bank statement	4,585
Add:	
Adera Ltd	2,198
Mist Northern	1,004
Total to add	3,202
Less:	
Lindstrom Co	846
HGW Ltd	3,200
Total to subtract	4,046
Balance as per cash book	3,741

 BPP

Chapter 3 – Introduction to control accounts

Task 3.1

(a)

Account	Amount £	Debit	Credit
Payables ledger control	3,390		3,390
VAT control	565	565	
Purchases	2,825	2,825	

(b)

Account	Amount £	Debit	Credit
Receivables ledger control	1,860		1,860
VAT control	310	310	
Sales returns	1,550	1,550	

(c)

Account	Amount £	Credit	Credit
Bank	4,590		4,590
Payables ledger control	4,590	4,590	

(d)

Account	Amount £	Debit	Credit
Bank	5,480	5,480	
Receivables ledger control	5,480		5,480

Task 3.2

Receivables ledger control

Details	Amount £	Details	Amount £
Balance b/f	11,689	Sales returns	1,582
Sales	12,758	Bank	11,563

Details	Amount £	Details	Amount £
		Discounts allowed	738
		Balance c/d	10,564
	24,447		24,447

Task 3.3

Payables ledger control

Details	Amount £	Details	Amount £
Purchases returns	728	Balance b/f	8,347
Bank	8,837	Purchases	9,203
Discounts received	382		
Balance c/d	7,603		
	17,550		17,550

Task 3.4

Payables ledger control account

Date	Details	Amount £	Date	Details	Amount £
30 June	Bank	33,106	1 June	Balance b/f	85,299
30 June	Discounts received	1,000	30 June	Purchases	39,300
30 June	Purchases returns	275			
30 June	Balance c/d	90,218			
		124,599			124,599
			1 July	Balance b/d	90,218

Task 3.5

(a) The correct answer is:

	✓
£32,125	✓
£33,975	
£34,725	
£33,225	

Working

	£
Brought forward balance (existing outstanding debt)	31,475
Sales	125,000
Less receipts	(122,500)
Less credit notes	(1,300)
Less discounts	(550)
Total	32,125

(b) The correct answer is:

	✓
£38,100	✓
£40,500	
£47,500	
£49,900	

Working

	£
Opening balance	34,500
Credit purchases	78,400
Discounts received	(1,200)
Payments	(68,900)
Purchases returns	(4,700)
	38,100

Task 3.6

(a)

Details	Amount £	Details	Amount £
VAT on purchases	2,500	Balance b/f	4,500
VAT on sales returns	300	VAT on sales	6,000
Payment to HMRC	7,000	VAT on purchase returns	250
Balance c/d	950		
	10,750		10,750
		Balance b/d	950

(b) £ 5,450

Balance b/d at 31 March 20XX of £950 plus the VAT of £4,500 on sales made during April

 BPP

ANSWERS

Chapter 4 – Preparing and reconciling control accounts

Task 4.1

The correct answers are:

	Control account ✓	List of balances ✓	Both ✓
Invoice entered into the sales daybook as £980 instead of £890			✓
Purchases daybook overcast by £1,000	✓		
Discounts allowed of £20 not entered into the cash book (debit side)			✓
An invoice taken as £340 instead of £440 when being posted to the customer's account		✓	
Incorrect balancing of a memorandum ledger account		✓	
A purchases return not entered into the purchases returns daybook			✓

Task 4.2

Receivables ledger control account

Details	Amount £	Details	Amount £
Balance b/f	5,000	Bank	11,900
Sales	9,600	Balance c/d	2,700
	14,600		14,600
Balance b/d	2,700		

Receivables ledger

H Simms

Details	Amount £	Details	Amount £
Balance b/f	900	Bank	2,400
Sales	2,000	Balance c/d	500
	2,900		2,900
Balance b/d	500		

P Good

Details	Amount £	Details	Amount £
Balance b/f	1,600	Bank	3,600
Sales	2,700	Balance c/d	700
	4,300		4,300
Balance b/d	700		

K Mitchell

Details	Amount £	Details	Amount £
Sales	1,100	Bank	1,100

C Brown

Details	Amount £	Details	Amount £
Balance b/f	2,500	Bank	4,800
Sales	3,800	Balance c/d	1,500
	6,300		6,300
Balance b/d	1,500		

Reconciliation of receivables ledger balances with the control account balance

	£
H Simms	500
P Good	700
K Mitchell	–
C Brown	1,500
Receivables ledger control account	2,700

Working

Sales (receivables ledger control) = (2,000 + 2,700 + 1,100 + 3,800) = 9,600

Bank (receivables ledger control) = (2,400 + 3,600 + 1,100 + 4,800) = 11,900

Task 4.3

Payables ledger control

Details	Amount £	Details	Amount £
Bank	7,900	Balance b/f	2,700
Balance c/d	2,100	Purchases	7,300
	10,000		10,000
		Balance b/d	2,100

Payables ledger

J Peters

Details	Amount £	Details	Amount £
Bank	1,700	Balance b/f	300
Balance c/d	200	Purchases	1,600
	1,900		1,900
		Balance b/d	200

T Sands

Details	Amount £	Details	Amount £
Bank	3,200	Balance b/f	1,700
Balance c/d	1,000	Purchases	2,500
	4,200		4,200
		Balance b/d	1,000

L Farmer

Details	Amount £	Details	Amount £
Bank	3,000	Balance b/f	700
Balance c/d	900	Purchases	3,200
	3,900		3,900
		Balance b/d	900

Reconciliation of payables ledger balances with control account balance

	£
J Peters	200
T Sands	1,000
L Farmer	900
Payables ledger control account	2,100

Working

Bank (payables ledger control) = 1,700 + 3,200 + 3,000 = 7,900

Purchases (payables ledger control) = 1,600 + 2,500 + 3,200 = 7,300

Task 4.4

(a)

Receivables ledger control

Details	Amount £	Details	Amount £
Balance b/f	9,450	Returns	700
Sales on credit	14,500	Bank	15,600
		Balance c/d	7,650
	23,950		23,950
Balance b/d	7,650		

(b) £ | 7,650 |

£90 which is the difference between the receivables ledger control account balance of £7,650 (balance b/d) and the total balances on the receivables ledger (3,000 + 1,250 + 3,310 = £7,650)

(c) The correct answers are:

	✓
A cash receipt was incorrectly entered onto the customer's account in the receivables ledger	✓
A sales invoice has been duplicated in the receivables ledger	
A sales return credit note has only been recorded in the receivables ledger control account	
Discounts have been posted twice in the customer's receivables ledger account	✓

 BPP

Response Option	Explanation
A cash receipt was incorrectly entered onto the customer's account in the receivables ledger	As the receivables ledger is lower than the receivables ledger control account, it is possible that a cash receipt was incorrectly entered onto the customer account.
A sales invoice has been duplicated in the receivables ledger	This would increase the receivables ledger, so that the receivables ledger would be GREATER than the receivables ledger control.
A sales return credit note has only been recorded in the receivables ledger control account	This would reduce the receivables ledger control account, so that the receivables ledger would be GREATER than the receivables ledger control.
Discounts have been posted twice in the customer's receivables ledger account	As the receivables ledger is lower than the receivables ledger control account, it is possible that discounts have been duplicated on the customer account.

Task 4.5

(a)

Payables ledger control

Details	Amount	Details	Amount
	£		£
Bank	9,750	Balance b/f	12,500
Discounts received	500	Purchases	8,600
Balance c/d	10,850		
	21,100		21,100
		Balance b/d	10,850

(b)

	£
Payables ledger control account balance as at 31 July 20XX	10,850
Total of the payables ledger accounts as at 31 July 20XX	10,650
Difference	200

(c) The correct answer is:

	✓
Purchases on credit have been recorded on the debit side of the payables ledger	✓
A purchase invoice has been duplicated in the payables ledger	
Discounts received have been omitted from the payables ledger but recorded in the payables ledger control account	
A cash payment to a credit supplier has been booked to the payables ledger control account only	

Response Option	Explanation
Purchases on credit have been recorded on the debit side of the payables ledger	This would decrease the balance on the payables ledger, therefore making it less than the control account balance
A purchase invoice has been duplicated in the payables ledger	This would increase the balance on the payables ledger
Discounts received have been omitted from the payables ledger but recorded in the payables ledger control account	This makes the balance on the payables ledger control account lower than that on the payables ledger
A cash payment to a credit supplier has been booked to the payables ledger control account only	This makes the balance on the payables ledger control account lower than that on the payables ledger

Task 4.6

(a)

Receivables ledger control

Date	Details	Amount £	Date	Details	Amount £
01 Nov	Balance b/f	48,125	30 Nov	Bank	28,327
30 Nov	Sales	37,008	30 Nov	Discounts allowed	240
			30 Nov	Sales returns	2,316
			30 Nov	Balance c/d	54,250
		85,133			85,133
01 Dec	Balance b/d	54,250			

 BPP

(b)

	£
Receivables ledger control account balance as at 1 December	54,250
Total of receivables ledger accounts as at 1 December	54,163
Difference	87

(c) The correct answers are:

	✓
VAT has been overstated on an invoice.	
VAT has been understated on an invoice.	
A sales invoice has been entered in the receivables ledger twice.	
A sales credit note has been entered in the receivables ledger twice.	✓
A receipt from a customer has been omitted from the receivables ledger.	
A receipt from a customer has been entered in the receivables ledger twice.	✓

Task 4.7

(a)

Transactions	Amount	VAT
	£	£
Sales on credit including VAT at 20%	106,800	17,800
Purchases on credit including VAT at 20%	54,000	9,000
Credit notes issued including VAT at 20%	2,820	470

(b)

VAT control

Details	Amount	Details	Amount
	£		£
Sales returns	470	Sales	17,800
Purchases	9,000		
Balance c/d	8,330		
	17,800		17,800
		Balance b/d	8,330

(c) £ 8,330

Task 4.8

(a) The correct answer is:

	✓
The receivables ledger control account shows a difference to the receivables ledger account balances	
Sales were less than purchases for the quarter	✓
There was an underpayment of VAT in the previous quarter	

A difference on the receivables ledger control account would have no impact on the VAT due, and an underpayment of VAT in the prior period would not result in a repayment from HMRC.

(b) £ 21,540

Working

£129,240 × 20/120 = £21,540

Task 4.9

(a) The correct answer is:

	✓
The supplier sent an invoice for £150 which you have not yet received	
The supplier has given you £150 settlement discount which you had not entered in your ledger	✓
You have paid the supplier £150 which he has not yet accounted for	
You have returned goods worth £150 which the supplier has not yet accounted for	

All other options would lead to a higher balance in the supplier's records.

(b) The correct answer is:

	✓
The control account only	
The list of balances only	
Both the control account and the list of balances	✓

(c)

Amount £	Debit ✓	Credit ✓
46,167		✓

Working

	£		£
Debit entries	24,500	Credit entries	76,961
SO Payment	1,606		
Correction (need to remove from PLCA)	4,688		
Balance c/d	46,167		
	76,961		76,961

Once the balance is brought down at the start of the next period, it appears in the credit column

Task 4.10

(a) The correct answers are:

	✓
The balance on the bank statement	
The balance on the receivables ledger control account	✓
The balance on the payables ledger control account	
The total of all the payables ledger balances	
The total of all the receivables ledger balances	✓

(b) The correct answer is:

	✓
How much is owed to suppliers at any point	
Over how many months the outstanding balance owed by each individual credit customer has built up	✓
The total purchases over the year to date to each credit supplier	

Task 4.11

(a)

Account name	Amount £	Debit ✓	Credit ✓
Irrecoverable debts	1,560	✓	
VAT control	312	✓	
Receivables ledger control	1,872		✓

 BPP

(b)

VAT control account

Details	Amount £	Details	Amount £
		Balance b/f	250
Purchases	90	Sales	1,400
Sales returns	50		
Irrecoverable debt expense	312		
Balance c/d	1,198		
	1,650		1,650
		Balance b/d	1,198

Task 4.12

Journal

Account name	Amount £	Debit ✓	Credit ✓
Irrecoverable debt expense	240	✓	
VAT control	48	✓	
Receivables ledger control	288		✓

Working

VAT control amount = (£240 × 20%) = £48

Task 4.13

Account name	Amount £	Debit ✓	Credit ✓
Irrecoverable debt expense	1,975	✓	
VAT control	395	✓	
Receivables ledger control	2,370		✓

 BPP

Chapter 5 – The journal

Task 5.1

Journal

Account name	Debit £	Credit £
Capital		10,000
Furniture and fittings	15,315	
Motor vehicles	20,109	
Cash at bank	15,000	
Payables ledger control		37,238
Receivables ledger control	12,524	
Loan from bank		7,000
VAT (owed to HM Revenue & Customs)		8,710
Totals	62,948	62,948

Task 5.2

Account name	Amount £	Debit ✓	Credit ✓
Petty cash	200	✓	
Bank	300	✓	
Capital	500		✓
Van	6,000	✓	
Trade receivables	7,700	✓	
Loan from bank	9,000		✓
VAT control (owed to HM Revenue & Customs)	1,300		✓
Trade payables	3,400		✓

Task 5.3

Account name	Amount £	Debit ✓	Credit ✓
Cash	150	✓	

Account name	Amount £	Debit ✓	Credit ✓
Cash at bank	12,350	✓	
Capital	23,456		✓
Fixtures and fittings	2,100	✓	
Trade receivables	3,206	✓	
Loan from bank	10,000		✓
Motor vehicle	15,650	✓	

Task 5.4

(a) £ 1,761

Working

	£
Gross wages	2,200
Income tax	(256)
Employees' NIC	(183)
Net wages	1,761

(b)

Wages expense

Details	Amount £	Details	Amount £
Wages control	2,200		
Wages control	200		

Wages control

Details	Amount £	Details	Amount £
Bank	1,761	Wages expense	2,200
HMRC control	183	Wages expense	200
HMRC control	256		
HMRC control	200		

HMRC control

Details	Amount £	Details	Amount £
		Wages control	200
		Wages control	256
		Wages control	183

Bank

Details	Amount £	Details	Amount £
		Wages control	1,761

Task 5.5

The correct answers are:

	Employee ✓	HMRC ✓	Pension company ✓	Employer ✓
Income Tax		✓		
NIC (employee)		✓		
Pension contributions			✓	
Net wages	✓			

Task 5.6

(a) £ 140

Working

£3,500 × 0.04

(b) £ 2,605

Working

Net wages is £2,605 (3,500 – 200 – 500 – 180 – 15)

(c)

Journal

Details	Debit £	Credit £
Wages control	340	
Pension administrator		340

Working

Wages control debit = 200 + 140 = 340

(d)

Journal

Details	Debit £	Credit £
Wages control	15	
Trade union subscription		15

(e)

Details	Debit £	Credit £
Bank		2,605
Wages control	2,605	

(f) £ 3,850

Working

Gross wages of £3,500 + Employer NIC of £210 + Pension contributions of 4% of gross wages of £140

Task 5.7

Date	Nominal Code	Debit £	Credit £
31 March	8000 – Gross wages	14,168	
31 March	8004 – Employer NI	240	
31 March	1220 – PAYE		823
31 March	1221 – National Insurance		1,021
31 March	1220 – Net wages		12,564

 BPP

Chapter 6 – Initial trial balance

Task 6.1

Ledger account	Balance	Debit ✓	Credit ✓
Sales	592,513		✓
Telephone	1,295	✓	
Receivables ledger control	52,375	✓	
Wages	104,288	✓	
Purchases returns	8,229		✓
Bank overdraft	17,339		✓
Purchases	372,589	✓	
Drawings	71,604	✓	
Sales returns	32,800	✓	
Car	14,700	✓	
Payables ledger control	31,570		✓

Task 6.2

	£	Debit £	Credit £
Office equipment		36,440	
Purchases		196,800	
Motor vehicles	76,800	76,800	
Sales	285,600		285,600
Bank (overdraft)	2,016		2,016
Petty cash	36	36	
Capital	90,000		90,000
Sales returns	5,640	5,640	
Purchases returns	4,320		4,320
Receivables ledger control	42,960	42,960	
Payables ledger control	36,120		36,120
VAT (owed to HMRC)	15,540		15,540
Drawings	12,040	12,040	
Telephone	1,920	1,920	
Electricity	3,360	3,360	

	£	Debit £	Credit £
Wages	74,520	74,520	
Loan from bank	36,000		36,000
Discounts allowed	7,680	7,680	
Discounts received	4,680		4,680
Rent expense	16,080	16,080	
Totals		474,276	474,276

Task 6.3

The correct answer is:

Debit balances	Credit balances	✓
Assets and income	Liabilities, capital and expenses	
Income, capital and liabilities	Assets and expenses	
Assets and expenses	Liabilities, capital and income	✓
Assets, expenses and capital	Liabilities and income	

Task 6.4

The correct answer is:

	✓
An asset or an expense	
A liability or an expense	
An amount owing to the organisation	
A liability or income	✓

Task 6.5

The correct answer is:

	✓
Non-current assets	
Sales returns	
Discounts allowed	
Bank overdraft	✓

ANSWERS

Task 6.6

	£	Debit £	Credit £
Bank (overdraft)	4,838		4,838
Capital	216,000		216,000
Discounts allowed	18,432	18,432	
Discounts received	11,232		11,232
Drawings	28,896	28,896	
Electricity	8,064	8,064	
Loan from bank	86,400		86,400
Motor vehicles	184,320	184,320	
Office equipment	87,456	87,456	
Petty cash	100	100	
Purchases	472,320	472,320	
Payables ledger control	86,688		86,688
Purchases returns	10,368		10,368
Rent expense	38,592	38,592	
Sales	685,440		685,440
Receivables ledger control	103,104	103,104	
Sales returns	13,536	13,536	
Telephone	4,608	4,608	
VAT (owed to HMRC)	37,310		37,310
Wages	178,848	178,848	
Totals		1,138,276	1,138,276

Chapter 7 – Errors and the trial balance

Task 7.1

(a)

Journal to remove the incorrect entry

Account name	Debit £	Credit £
Sales	3,750	

Journal to record the correct entry

Account name	Debit £	Credit £
Sales		3,570

Journal to remove the suspense account balance

Account name	Debit £	Credit £
Suspense		180

(b)

Journal to remove the incorrect entries

Account name	Debit £	Credit £
Drawings	350	
Cash		350

Journal to record the correct entries

Account name	Debit £	Credit £
Drawings	350	
Cash		350

Task 7.2

Account name	Amount	Debit ✓	Credit ✓
Suspense	11,081	✓	

Task 7.3

The correct answer is:

	✓
A credit note from a supplier with a net amount of £124 was not entered in the payables ledger	
Discounts allowed of £124 were only posted to the discounts allowed account	✓
A cash purchase for £124 was not entered in the purchases account	
An irrecoverable debt write-off of £124 was not entered in the subsidiary ledger	

The credit note and irrecoverable debt omissions affect only the subsidiary ledgers, so would not cause a suspense account balance. Omitting the cash purchase from the purchases account would lead to a debit balance on the suspense account, not a credit balance. The correction for the discount error is to credit the receivables ledger control account and debit suspense, thus clearing the credit balance on the suspense account.

Task 7.4

(a)

Journal to remove the incorrect entry

Account name	Debit £	Credit £
VAT control		582

Journal to record the correct entry

Account name	Debit £	Credit £
VAT control	528	

Journal to remove the suspense account balance

Account name	Debit £	Credit £
Suspense	54	

(b)

Journal to remove the incorrect entries

Account name	Debit £	Credit £
Purchases	800	
Cash		800

Journal to record the correct entries

Account name	Debit	Credit
	£	£
Purchases	800	
Cash		800

Task 7.5

(a)

Journal to remove the incorrect entry

Account name	Debit	Credit
	£	£
Sales returns		6,475

Journal to record the correct entry

Account name	Debit	Credit
	£	£
Sales returns	6,745	

Journal to remove the suspense account balance

Account name	Debit	Credit
	£	£
Suspense		270

(b)

Journal to remove the incorrect entries

Account name	Debit	Credit
	£	£
Bank	450	
Receivables ledger control		450

Journal to record the correct entries

Account name	Debit	Credit
	£	£
Bank	450	
Receivables ledger control		450

 BPP

Task 7.6

The journals

(a)

Details	Debit £	Credit £
Sales returns	500	
Sales		500

(b)

Details	Debit £	Credit £
Office expenses	125	
Bank		125
Office expenses	125	
Bank		125

(c)

Details	Debit £	Credit £
Bank	29	
Suspense	270	
Purchases		299
Purchases	299	
Bank		299

(d)

Details	Debit £	Credit £
Receivables ledger control	388	
Suspense		388
Discounts allowed	388	
Receivables ledger control		388

Task 7.7

Suspense

Date	Details	Amount £	Date	Details	Amount £
01 July	Sales	945	30 June	Balance b/f	720
			01 July	Rent and rates	225
		945			945

Task 7.8

(a) The correct answer is:

	✓
Debit £90	
Credit £90	✓
Debit £1,780	
Credit £1,780	

£890 should have been debited to the expense account. Instead, £980 has been debited. To bring this amount down to £890, the expense account should be credited with £90.

(b) The correct answer is:

	✓
Error of transposition	
Error of omission	✓
Error of principle	
Error of commission	

(c) The correct answer is:

	✓
A transaction has not been recorded	
One side of a transaction has been recorded in the wrong account, and that account is of a different class to the correct account	
One side of a transaction has been recorded in the wrong account, and that account is of the same class as the correct account	✓
A transaction has been recorded using the wrong amount	

ANSWERS

(d) The correct answer is:

	✓
A gas bill credited to the gas account and debited to the bank account	
The purchase of a non-current asset credited to the asset account and debited to the supplier's account	
The purchase of a non-current asset debited to the purchases account and credited to the supplier's account	✓
The payment of wages debited and credited to the correct accounts, but using the wrong amount	

Task 7.9

(a) The correct answer is:

	✓
Omission	
Original entry	✓
Commission	
Principle	

(b) The correct answer is:

	✓
Debit £1,350	✓
Credit £1,350	
Debit £13,650	
Credit £13,650	

Working

Suspense account

Details	Amount £	Details	Amount £
Opening balance	1,350	Discounts allowed	7,500
Discounts received	6,150		
	7,500		7,500

(c) The correct answer is:

	✓
The credit side to be £48 more than the debit side	
The debit side to be £48 more than the credit side	
The credit side to be £96 more than the debit side	
The debit side to be £96 more than the credit side	✓

Working

Debits will exceed credits by 2 × £48 = £96

(d) The correct answers are:

	Yes ✓	No ✓
Omitting both entries for a transaction		✓
Posting the debit entry for an invoice to an incorrect expense account		✓
Omitting the debit entry for a transaction	✓	
Posting the debit entry for a transaction as a credit entry	✓	

Task 7.10

The correct answers are:

Error in the general ledger	Error disclosed by the trial balance ✓	Error NOT disclosed by the trial balance ✓
Recording a bank receipt of a cash sale on the debit side of the cash sales account	✓	
Entering an insurance expense in the administration expenses account		✓
Entering the discounts received account balance on the debit side of the trial balance	✓	
Miscasting the total column of one page of the sales returns daybook	✓	
Failing to write up a dishonoured cheque in the cash book		✓
Recording discount allowed of £15 as £150 in the cash book		✓

Task 7.11

Discounts allowed

Details	Amount £	Details	Amount
Suspense	209		

Machinery

Details	Amount	Details	Amount
		Motor vehicles	4,300

Motor vehicles

Details	Amount £	Details	Amount £
Machinery	4,300		

Receivables ledger control

Details	Amount £	Details	Amount £
		Suspense	750

Suspense

Details	Amount £	Details	Amount £
Receivables ledger control	750	Balance b/f	541
		Discounts allowed	209

Task 7.12

	Balances extracted on 30 June £	Balances at 1 July Debit £	Balances at 1 July Credit £
Machinery	82,885	82,885	
Computer equipment	41,640	41,640	
Insurance	17,520	17,520	
Bank (overdraft)	13,252		13,252

	Balances extracted on 30 June	Balances at 1 July Debit	Balances at 1 July Credit
	£	£	£
Petty cash	240	240	
Receivables ledger control	241,500	247,250	
Payables ledger control	134,686		134,686
VAT (owing to HM Revenue and Customs)	19,920		19,920
Capital	44,826		44,826
Sales	525,092		525,092
Purchases	269,400	269,400	
Purchases returns	16,272		16,272
Wages	61,680	61,680	
Maintenance expenses	3,283	3,283	
Stationery	8,049	8,049	
Rent and rates	3,466	3,466	
Heat and light	5,172	5,712	
Telephone	7,596	7,596	
Marketing expenses	5,327	5,327	
Totals		754,048	754,048

Working

Workings to the answer (for information only)

Suspense

Details	Amount	Details	Amount
	£		£
Balance b/f	6,290	Receivables ledger control	2,875
Heat and light	5,172	Receivables ledger control	2,875
		Heat and light	5,712
	11,462		11,462

Heat & Light

Details	Amount	Details	Amount
	£		£
Balance b/f	5,172	Suspense	5,172

Details	Amount £	Details	Amount £
Suspense	5,712	Balance c/d	5,712

Receivables ledger control

Details	Amount £	Details	Amount £
Balance b/f	241,500		
Suspense	2,875		
Suspense	2,875	Balance c/d	247,250
	247,250		247,250

Task 7.13

(a) (i)

Account name	Amount £	Debit ✓	Credit ✓
VAT	1,100		✓

(ii)

Account name	Amount £	Debit ✓	Credit ✓
VAT	1,000	✓	

(iii)

Account name	Amount £	Debit ✓	Credit ✓
Suspense	100	✓	

(b) (i)

Account name	Amount £	Debit ✓	Credit ✓
Heat and light	350	✓	
Bank	350		✓

(ii)

Account name	Amount £	Debit ✓	Credit ✓
Heat and light	350	✓	
Bank	350		✓

AAT Q2022
Practice Assessment

Principles of Bookkeeping Controls

You are advised to attempt practice assessments online from the AAT website. This will ensure you are prepared for how the assessment will be presented on the AAT's system when you attempt the real assessment. Please access the assessment using the address below:

https://www.aat.org.uk/training/study-support/search

The AAT may call the assessments on their website, under study support resources, either a 'practice assessment' or 'sample assessment'.

BPP Practice Assessment 1

Principles of Bookkeeping Controls

Time allowed: 1 hour 30 minutes

Principles of Bookkeeping Controls
BPP Practice Assessment 1

Assessment information

You have **1 hour and 30 minutes** to complete this practice assessment.

This assessment contains **8 tasks** and you should attempt to complete **every** task.

Each task is independent. You will not need to refer to your answers to previous tasks.

The total number of marks for this assessment is **80**.

Read every task carefully to make sure you understand what is required.

Where the date is relevant, it is given in the task data.

Both minus signs and brackets can be used to indicate negative numbers **unless** task instructions state otherwise.

You must use a full stop to indicate a decimal point. For example, write 100.57 **not** 100,57 **or** 10057.

You may use a comma to indicate a number in the thousands, but you don't have to. For example, 10000 and 10,000 are both acceptable.

Mathematical rounding should be applied where appropriate.

Task 1 (10 marks)

This task is about using control accounts.

A receivables ledger control account balance is shown in the general ledger.

Required

(a) Identify which ONE of the following is correct in relation to the receivables ledger control account.

	✓
A receivables ledger control account enables quick identification of the total amount owed to the business by customers.	
A receivables ledger control account enables quick identification of an amount owed by a specific customer.	
A receivables ledger control account should always be produced by the same person who produces the subsidiary ledgers as this improves accuracy.	
A receivables ledger control account enables discrepancies between the bank and the subsidiary ledger to be quickly identified.	

(1 mark)

You work in the accounts department of Arnolia Ltd. Your manager has run a report which shows a credit balance on the VAT control account at the end of April of £3,220. The credit balance at the end of March was £8,300. Your manager has asked you to prepare a VAT control account to explain why April shows a lower balance.

The following information has been recorded during the month of April:

	Amount £
VAT on sales	4,600
VAT on purchases	2,200
VAT on sales returns	140
VAT on purchases returns	90
VAT on discounts allowed	20
VAT on discounts received	20
VAT on cash sales	170
Payment made to HMRC	7,600

Required

(b) Complete the VAT control account below for April by selecting an entry from each pick list and entering amounts in the spaces provided. You must ensure a number is entered in each space provided.

VAT Control Account

Details	Amount £	Details	Amount £
		Balance b/d	8,300
▼		▼	
▼		▼	
▼		▼	
▼		▼	
Balance c/d	3,220		

Picklist

- Bank
- Cash sales
- Discounts allowed
- Discounts received
- Purchases
- Purchases returns
- Sales
- Sales returns

(8 marks)

Victoria Ltd has the following receivables ledger control account.

Receivables Ledger Control Account

Date	Details	Amount £	Date	Details	Amount £
1/05	Balance b/d	8,470	31/05	Sales returns	920
31/05	Sales	52,000	31/05	Bank	29,860
			31/05	Discounts allowed	940
			31/05	Balance c/d	

Required

(c) What will be the balance carried down on the receivables ledger control account?

£ [   ]

(1 mark)

Task 2 (10 marks)

This task is about reconciling control accounts.

The balance on the payables ledger control account will appear in the year-end trial balance. It is important to reconcile this to the payables ledger.

BPP

Required

(a) Identify which ONE of the following statements is a reason for completing this reconciliation.

	✓
The payables ledger is always more accurate than the payables ledger control account.	
Errors in the payables ledger or payables ledger control account can be identified and corrected.	
The payables ledger can be deleted once it has been reconciled which helps to keep record keeping simple.	
Any errors can be identified and included in the suspense account balance.	

(1 mark)

You work in the accounts department of Pao Ltd. You have been asked to reconcile the balance on the payables ledger control account to your suppliers report.

The following suppliers report as at 31 October has been provided.

Supplier name	Reference	Balance owed £	Payment terms Days
Pallets 2 U Ltd	PA001	29,739	30
HMRC	HMRC	7,264	30
Cable Reels Ltd	CA001	7,108	30
Brick Dust Ltd	BR001	6,746	30
Cable Drums Ltd	CA002	5,845	30
Nice Mice Ltd	NI001	937	30
Rustic Runes Ltd	RU001	648	30
Lost and Found Ltd	LO001	276	30

Required

(b) (i) If the payables ledger control account reconciles with the payables ledger, what will be the balance?

£ [   ]   (2 marks)

The balance on the payables ledger control account is £57,930.

Required

(ii) Complete the following statement:

The payables ledger control account is £ [   ] [▼] than the payables ledger.

Picklist

- Less
- More

(2 marks)

At Zen Ltd the payables ledger control account shows a balance of £67,697 but the individual balances in the payables ledger only add up to £65,327.

Required

(c) Identify whether each of the following may explain the difference between the two balances.

Reason	May explain the difference ✓	Does not explain the difference ✓
A purchase from a new supplier was missed from the list of individual balances when totalling the payables ledger.		
A purchase invoice has been recorded twice in the payables ledger.		
A cash purchase has not been recorded.		
A transposition error was made when recording a purchase invoice in the purchases daybook.		
A discount received from a supplier has been recorded twice in the individual supplier account in the payables ledger.		

(5 marks)

Task 3 (4 marks)

This task is about payment methods and reconciling the cash book to the bank statement.

Required

(a) Match ONE payment method to each description by selecting the appropriate option from the pick list provided.

Description	Payment method
A payment made by card which may be paid off in part at the end of the month.	▼
A payment method used to make the same regular payment to the bank account of a third party.	▼
A method of making regular payments to the bank account of a third party which can vary in amount.	▼
A payment method used for low-value transactions, which must be counted before being banked.	▼

Picklist

- BACS
- CHAPS
- Cash
- Cheque
- Credit card
- Debit card

 BPP

- Direct debit
- Standing Order

A business is reconciling its bank statement to its cash book balance.

Required

(b) Identify which ONE of the following statements is true.

	✓
The balance on the bank statement will almost always agree with the balance on the cash book.	
There is often a time delay between transactions being entered in both the cash book and the bank statement, resulting in differences in the balance per the cash book and the balance per the bank statement.	
An outstanding lodgement is a cheque payment which has not yet appeared on the bank statement.	

(1 mark)

(c) Identify whether each of the following statements are true or false.

Statement	True ✓	False ✓
Comparing the debit side of the cash book to the amounts paid out in the bank statement will enable any automated payments that have been missed in the cash book to be identified.		
A direct debit of £67 for the business' broadband connection is shown in the bank statement. This is not in the cash book. £67 will need to be added in the bank reconciliation to make it agree to the cash book.		
Direct debits, bank charges and unpresented cheques are all examples of timing differences		

(3 marks)

Task 4 (12 marks)

This task is about reconciling a bank statement with the cash book.

The cash book for Samuel's firework business at 30 June is shown below. Samuel pays all of his suppliers by cheque. His customers pay him by either cheque or bank transfer.

Cash book

Date 20XX	Details	Bank £	Date 20XX	Details	Bank £
1 Jun	Balance b/d	6,988	5 Jun	Dyna Ltd	2,232
6 Jun	K Haque	324	13 Jun	Fire Safety Ltd	1,943
12 Jun	C Smith	1,456	27 Jun	Guido Ltd	120
19 Jun	M Singh	2,435			

 BPP

Date 20XX	Details	Bank £	Date 20XX	Details	Bank £
28 Jun	I Lopez	325		Balance c/d	7,233

The bank statement for the same period is as follows:

Date 20XX	Details	Paid in £	Paid out £	Balance £
1 June	Balance			6,750
2 June	Cheque – S Jones	678		7,428
6 June	Transfer – Haque KM	324		7,752
7 June	Cheque 007821		2,232	5,520
12 June	Cheque 007820		440	5,080
12 June	Transfer – Smith C	1,456		6,536
23 June	Cheque – Singh M	2,435		8,971
28 June	Direct Debit – Electric Co		130	8,841
28 June	Cheque 007823		120	8,721
30 June	Bank charges		13	8,708
30 June	Transfer – W Smithers	560		9,268

Required

Update the cash book and prepare a bank reconciliation at 30 June.

Cash book		Debit £	Credit £
Closing balance b/d		7,233	
Adjustments:			
(1)	▼		
(1)	▼		
(1)	▼		
Adjusted balance c/d			

Picklist 1

- Bank charges
- Cheque 007820
- Cheque 007821
- Cheque 007823
- Cheque – S Jones

- Cheque – Singh M
- Direct Debit – Electric Co
- Transfer – Haque KM
- Transfer – Smith C
- Transfer – W Smithers

Bank reconciliation		£
Closing balance per bank statement		9,268
Add:		
(2)	▼	
Less:		
(2)	▼	
Adjusted closing balance		

Picklist 2

- C Smith
- Dyna Ltd
- Fire Safety Ltd
- Guido Ltd
- I Lopez
- K Haque
- M Singh

(12 marks)

Task 5 (10 marks)

This task is about using the journal.

Required

(a) **Identify which TWO of the following situations would be a correct use of the journal.**

	✓
Alex thinks he may have spent at least £300 more on entertaining bills than is currently showing on the entertaining expense account. He will, therefore, process an extra £300 debit via the journal.	
Nicki has reviewed her receivables listing and has identified a customer who owes £300. The debt is two years overdue and the customer is no longer trading. Nicki wishes to write the balance off.	
Mike has noticed his repairs and maintenance expense balance is much larger than he would expect and, on investigation, he identifies that an asset acquired for £4,000 has been incorrectly coded to repairs and maintenance. He wishes to correct this by debiting the asset and crediting the expense.	
Hannah is selling her business and wants to leave the purchaser detailed notes on how the business works. She will record these in the journal.	

(2 marks)

A journal has been recorded in the accounting system as follows.

Journal date: 30 September		Journal number: 52		
Number	Account	Debit £	Credit £	Description
1	Payroll liabilities: employees		17,235	Net pay
2	Payroll expenses – wages	20,979		Gross pay
3	Payroll expenses – taxes	1,564		National insurance employer
4	Payroll liabilities: HMRC		1,946	PAYE
5	Payroll liabilities: HMRC		1,798	National insurance employee
6	Payroll liabilities: HMRC		1,564	National insurance employer

Prior to this journal, the balance on the Payroll liabilities: HMRC account was a debit balance of £59.00.

Required

(b) After the journals are processed, what will be the revised balance on the Payroll liabilities: HMRC account?

£ [   ]

(2 marks)

The following invoice has been outstanding for more than six months and Martin wishes to write off the amount as an irrecoverable debt.

Martin's Roofing 7 Big Street Oxford OX1 3DO VAT ref: 737439575			**Bill to:** Mr and Mrs Little 2 Middle Street Abingdon OX8 9QP Invoice no: 00057 Date: 1 May 20X0 Due: 31 May 20X0 Terms: Payment 30 days from date of invoice	
Date	Description	VAT	Quantity	Amount £
1 May X0	Roof tile replacement	20%	1	780
		Total		780
		VAT		156
		Amount Due		936

Required

(c) Complete the journal entries below to record the irrecoverable debt write off in the nominal ledger. You should select the account name from the picklist and then include the appropriate amount in either the Debit or Credit column of the journal entry.

 BPP

Date of journal: 31 December Journal number: 002			
Account name	Debit £	Credit £	Description
▼			Write off irrecoverable debt
▼			Write off irrecoverable debt
▼			Write off irrecoverable debt

Picklist

- Discounts allowed
- Irrecoverable debt expense
- Payables ledger control account
- Receivables ledger control account
- VAT control account

(6 marks)

Task 6 (10 marks)

This task is about using the journal to correct errors.

A suspense account is shown in the trial balance of Rachel's business.

Required

(a) Identify which TWO of the following statements about suspense accounts are true.

	✓
The suspense account must not remain in the ledger accounts but may be allowed to remain in the trial balance.	
An error of reversal will give rise to a suspense account balance.	
The suspense account is created as a temporary measure in order to enable the initial trial balance to balance.	
A balance omission error will give rise to a suspense account balance.	

(2 marks)

(b) Identify whether each of the errors described below would or would not be disclosed by the trial balance.

Errors	Disclosed by the trial balance ✓	Not disclosed by the trial balance ✓
Avinesh posted only one side of the journal entry to write off an irrecoverable receivable.		
Yu Kay recorded a payment from a customer as £450 when in fact it should have been for £540.		

(2 marks)

Vicki and Barbara run a small business that specialises in sewing badges for children's school uniforms. They operate a manual accounting system and have prepared a trial balance at the year end. The trial balance shows debits of £18,384 and credits of £21,341.

They have identified the following errors:

- Error 1: The total on the sales daybook was £1,492. When processing this to the general ledger, Vicki credited both the sales account and the receivables ledger control account.

- Error 2: In May, Barbara paid a gas bill. She correctly credited the cash book with £125, but she recorded this as a debit in the utilities expense account as £152.

Required

(c) (i) **What is the balance on the suspense account in the trial balance?**

£ [   ] [▼]

Picklist

- Credit
- Debit

(2 marks)

(ii) **Complete the table below to show the debits and credits that will be processed to clear the suspense account.**

Date of journal: 31 December			Journal number: 73
Account name	Debit £	Credit £	Description
▼	2,984		Correction of Error 1
▼		2,984	Correction of Error 1
▼	27		Correction of Error 2
▼		27	Correction of Error 2

Picklist

- Bank
- Receivables ledger control account
- Sales
- Suspense
- Utilities expense

(4 marks)

Task 7 (10 marks)

This task is about extracting a trial balance.

Alberto runs a shop. Most of the ledger accounts have been closed off and the balances included in the trial balance as at 30 June.

Required

(a) **Complete the remaining ledger accounts by inserting the balance carried down on each account. Enter your answers to two decimal places.**

Bank:

Date 20XX	Details	Amount £	Date 20XX	Details	Amount £
1 Jun	Balance b/d	52,345.24	23 Jun	Purchases	11,532.22
5 Jun	Sales	7,389.34	25 Jun	Rent	769.00
24 Jun	Sales	3,000.00	30 Jun	Payables ledger control	52,095.24
30 Jun	Balance c/d				

VAT Control

Date 20XX	Details	Amount £	Date 20XX	Details	Amount £
6 Jun	Purchases	9,346.30	1 Jun	Balance b/d	364.33
			2 Jun	Sales	12,636.87
30 Jun	Balance c/d				

Discounts allowed:

Date 20XX	Details	Amount £	Date 20XX	Details	Amount £
1 Jun	Balance b/d	0.00			
30 Jun	Receivables ledger control	366.83			
			30 Jun	Balance c/d	

Payables ledger control:

Date 20XX	Details	Amount £	Date 20XX	Details	Amount £
30 Jun	Bank	52,095.24	1 Jun	Balance b/d	14,534.57
			23 Jun	Purchases	44,656.42
			28 Jun	Purchases	163.00
30 Jun	Balance c/d				

(4 marks)

(b) Complete the trial balance by inserting the missing figures and calculating the total for each column. Enter your answers to two decimal places.

	Debit £	Credit £
Sales		66,035.34
Purchases	42,695.57	
Rent	769.00	
Insurance	2,453.91	
Bank		
VAT Control		
Payables ledger control		
Receivables ledger control	32,325.56	
Discounts allowed		
Totals		

(6 marks)

Task 8 (10 marks)

This task is about redrafting a trial balance.

The initial list of balances for Elsa's business at 31 March is:

Item	£
Sales	71,466.02
Purchases	45,343.33
Discounts received	964.34
Bank	12,353.56
Plant and equipment	6,354.47
Receivables ledger control	3,435.56

Some errors have been identified and the following journals are required to be processed:

Date of journal: 31 March				Journal number: 056
Date	Description	Debit £	Credit £	Description
31 March	Purchases	4,972.68		Purchase of £2,486.34 recorded on credit side of payables account.
31 March	Suspense		4,972.68	Purchase of £2,486.34 recorded on credit side of payables account.
31 March	Suspense	29.24		Discount received not recorded in discount received account.

Date of journal: 31 March					Journal number: 056
Date	Description	Debit £	Credit £	Description	
31 March	Discounts received		29.24	Discount received not recorded in discount received account.	

Required

Complete the adjusted trial balance by inserting the correct figures in either the debit or credit column and entering totals for each column.

	Debit £	Credit £
Sales		
Purchases		
Discounts received		
Bank		
Plant and equipment		
Receivables ledger control		
Total		

(10 marks)

BPP Practice Assessment 1

Principles of Bookkeeping Controls

Answers

BPP

Task 1

(a) The correct answer is:

	✓
A receivables ledger control account enables quick identification of the total amount owed to the business by customers.	✓
A receivables ledger control account enables quick identification of an amount owed by a specific customer.	
A receivables ledger control account should always be produced by the same person who produces the subsidiary ledgers as this improves accuracy.	
A receivables ledger control account enables discrepancies between the bank and the subsidiary ledger to be quickly identified.	

A receivables ledger control account enables quick identification of the total amount owed to the business by customers.

The receivables ledger control account does not include the details of the specific customers from whom monies are owed, but only of the totals posted from the sales daybook.

It will not therefore allow quick identification of the amount owed by a specific customer because this information is only included in the receivables ledger account for that customer (subsidiary ledger).

The receivables ledger control account should ideally not be produced by the same person who produces the receivables subsidiary ledger accounts — it would be better to have segregation of duties between these two tasks in order to reduce the risk of fraud or error.

Finally, the receivables ledger control account does not help in the identification of discrepancies between the bank and the subsidiary ledger — discrepancies of this type would be more likely to be identified by performing a bank reconciliation.

(b)

VAT Control Account

Details	Amount £	Details	Amount £
		Balance b/d	8,300
Purchases	2,200	Sales	4,600
Sales returns	140	Purchases returns	90
Discounts allowed	20	Discounts received	20
Bank	7,600	Cash sales	170
Balance c/d	3,220		

To calculate the balance carried down, first total the debit and credit columns to identify the higher of the two sides. Here the credit column casts to £13,180 whereas the debit column casts to £9,960. The difference between the totals of £3,220 is the balance carried down. As the total of the debit side is the lower of the two columns, the balance carried down is shown on the debit side of the VAT Control Account so that the debit and credit columns balance.

(c) £ 28,750

= Total of debit entries − total of credit entries

= (£8,470 + £52,000) − (£920 + £29,860 + £940)

Task 2

(a) The correct answer is:

	✓
The payables ledger is always more accurate than the payables ledger control account.	
Errors in the payables ledger or payables ledger control account can be identified and corrected.	✓
The payables ledger can be deleted once it has been reconciled which helps to keep record keeping simple.	
Any errors can be identified and included in the suspense account balance.	

The payables ledger is not always more accurate than the control account – indeed, one of the purposes of keeping a control account is to help to identify errors in the payables ledger.

The payables ledger should not be deleted once it has been reconciled – it must be retained as part of the business' accounting records.

It is true that errors can be included in a suspense account balance, but this is not a reason for completing this reconciliation.

(b) (i) £ 58,563

This is the total of all of the balances owed. Since the control account is stated to reconcile with the payables ledger list of balances, this means that there are no adjusting items and that the total of the list of balances should be identical to the balance on the control account.

(ii) The payables ledger control account is £ 633 less than the payables ledger.

(= £58,563 − £57,930)

(c) The correct answers are:

Reason	May explain the difference ✓	Does not explain the difference ✓
A purchase from a new supplier was missed from the list of individual balances when totalling the payables ledger.	✓	
A purchase invoice has been recorded twice in the payables ledger.		✓
A cash purchase has not been recorded.		✓
A transposition error was made when recording a purchase invoice in the purchases daybook.		✓
A discount received from a supplier has been recorded twice in the individual supplier account in the payables ledger.	✓	

 BPP

Task 3

(a)

Description	Payment method
A payment made by card which may be paid off in part at the end of the month.	Credit card
A payment method used to make the same regular payment to the bank account of a third party.	Standing Order
A method of making regular payments to the bank account of a third party which can vary in amount.	Direct debit
A payment method used for low-value transactions, which must be counted before being banked.	Cash

(b) The correct answer is:

	✓
The balance on the bank statement will almost always agree with the balance on the cash book.	
There is often a time delay between transactions being entered in both the cash book and the bank statement, resulting in differences in the balance per the cash book and the balance per the bank statement.	✓
An outstanding lodgement is a cheque payment which has not yet appeared on the bank statement.	

There is often a time delay between transactions being entered in both the cash book and the bank statement, resulting in differences in the balance per the cash book and the balance per the bank statement.

This statement is true. Certain items may appear in either record first (eg interest tends to appear first in the bank statement, whereas cheque payments tend to appear first in the cash book). The bookkeeper will need to keep track of these items in order to reconcile the two balances.

The balance on the bank statement will very often not agree to that on the cash book — indeed, the frequency of the disagreement between the two figures is the purpose of performing a bank reconciliation.

An outstanding lodgement is money paid into the bank by the business but not yet appearing as a receipt on the bank statement — the question gives the definition of an unpresented cheque instead.

(c) The correct answers are:

Statement	True ✓	False ✓
Comparing the debit side of the cash book to the amounts paid out in the bank statement will enable any automated payments that have been missed in the cash book to be identified.		✓

 BPP

Statement	True ✓	False ✓
A direct debit of £67 for the business' broadband connection is shown in the bank statement. This is not in the cash book. £67 will need to be added in the bank reconciliation to make it agree to the cash book.	✓	
Direct debits, bank charges and unpresented cheques are all examples of timing differences		✓

The debit side of the cash book shows bank receipts, so this will not be related to bank payments (and therefore will not show any missed automated payments).

The direct debit here is a payment, which will have reduced the bank balance in the bank statement. This will need to be added to the bank statement balance for it to agree to the cash book.

Unpresented cheques are classified as a 'timing difference'; direct debits and bank charges are not timing differences, but items included on the bank statement that may have been missed from the cash book.

Task 4

Cash book	Debit £	Credit £
Closing balance b/d	7,233	
Adjustments:		
Direct Debit – Electric Co		130
Bank charges		13
Transfer – W Smithers	560	
Adjusted balance c/d		7,650

Bank reconciliation	£
Closing balance per bank statement	9,268
Add:	
I Lopez	325
Less:	
Fire Safety Ltd	1,943
Adjusted closing balance	7,650

Note that the two unmatched items on this month's bank statement (cheque receipt from S Jones £678 and cheque 007820 payment of £440) were recorded in last month's cash book. This explains the difference of £238 between the opening balance of the cash book (£6,988) and the opening balance of the bank statement (£6,750).

Task 5

(a) The correct answers are:

	✓
Alex thinks he may have spent at least £300 more on entertaining bills than is currently showing on the entertaining expense account. He will, therefore, process an extra £300 debit via the journal.	
Nicki has reviewed her receivables listing and has identified a customer who owes £300. The debt is two years overdue and the customer is no longer trading. Nicki wishes to write the balance off.	✓
Mike has noticed his repairs and maintenance expense balance is much larger than he would expect and, on investigation, he identifies that an asset acquired for £4,000 has been incorrectly coded to repairs and maintenance. He wishes to correct this by debiting the asset and crediting the expense.	✓
Hannah is selling her business and wants to leave the purchaser detailed notes on how the business works. She will record these in the journal.	

Regarding the incorrect options, Alex's intention to adjust the entertaining expense account because he merely thinks he may have spent more than is currently showing on the account is not a reason to use the journal.

In order to leave detailed notes for somebody, Hannah should use a means other than the accounting journal.

(b) £ 5,249

£1,946 + £1,798 + £1,564 − £59

(c)

Date of journal: 31 December	Journal number: 002		
Account name	Debit £	Credit £	Description
Receivables ledger control account		936	Write off irrecoverable debt
VAT control account	156		Write off irrecoverable debt
Irrecoverable debt expense	780		Write off irrecoverable debt

 BPP

Task 6

(a) The correct answers are:

	✓
The suspense account must not remain in the ledger accounts but may be allowed to remain in the trial balance.	
An error of reversal will give rise to a suspense account balance.	
The suspense account is created as a temporary measure in order to enable the initial trial balance to balance.	✓
A balance omission error will give rise to a suspense account balance.	✓

Regarding the incorrect options, it is true that the suspense account must not remain in the ledger accounts but it must also not remain in the trial balance.

An error of reversal will not give rise to a suspense account balance, because it simply means that the debit and credit entries have been posted to the wrong accounts (which does not mean that the figures were not equal).

(b) The correct answers are:

Errors	Disclosed by the trial balance ✓	Not disclosed by the trial balance ✓
Avinesh posted only one side of the journal entry to write off an irrecoverable receivable.	✓	
Yu Kay recorded a payment from a customer as £450 when in fact it should have been for £540.		✓

The first error would result in an imbalance between debits and credits (since if only one side of the journal were posted then only a debit or a credit entry can have been made). This would give rise to a balance on the suspense account.

The second error is an error of original entry, whereby the same amount was entered as a debit and as a credit, but the amount was incorrect. This does not result in a suspense account balance because debits and credits are the same.

(c) (i) £ 2,957   Debit

The suspense account balance is the difference between the total of the debit account balances (£18,384) and the total of the credit account balances (£21,341). The debit side is the lower of the two columns, hence the suspense account balance is a debit in the trial balance.

(ii)

Date of journal: 31 December			Journal number: 73
Account name	Debit £	Credit £	Description
Receivables ledger control account	2,984		Correction of Error 1

Date of journal: 31 December				Journal number: 73
Account name	Debit	Credit		Description
	£	£		
Suspense		2,984		Correction of Error 1
Suspense	27			Correction of Error 2
Utilities expense		27		Correction of Error 2

Error 1 resulted in a credit entry of £1,492 being posted to the receivables ledger control account instead of a debit entry. This meant that £1,492 × 2 was posted to the accounting records, on the credit side. Therefore, a debit of £2,984 was posted to the debit side of the suspense account to make the initial trial balance balance.

Error 1 is corrected by crediting suspense and debiting the receivables ledger control account.

Error 2 resulted in an excess £27 being debited to the expense account (£152 – £125). As the debit entries exceed the credit entries in respect of this transaction, £27 was credited to the suspense account.

Error 2 is corrected by crediting the utilities expense and debiting the suspense account, and thus clearing the balance.

Task 7

(a)

Bank:

Date 20XX	Details	Amount £	Date 20XX	Details	Amount £
1 Jun	Balance b/d	52,345.24	23 Jun	Purchases	11,532.22
5 Jun	Sales	7,389.34	25 Jun	Rent	769.00
24 Jun	Sales	3,000.00	30 Jun	Payables ledger control	52,095.24
30 Jun	Balance c/d	1,661.88			

VAT Control

Date 20XX	Details	Amount £	Date 20XX	Details	Amount £
6 Jun	Purchases	9,346.30	1 Jun	Balance b/d	364.33
			2 Jun	Sales	12,636.87
30 Jun	Balance c/d	3,654.90			

 BPP

Discounts allowed:

Date 20XX	Details	Amount £	Date 20XX	Details	Amount £
1 Jun	Balance b/d	0.00			
30 Jun	Receivables ledger control	366.83			
			30 Jun	Balance c/d	366.83

Payables ledger control:

Date 20XX	Details	Amount £	Date 20XX	Details	Amount £
30 Jun	Bank	52,095.24	1 Jun	Balance b/d	14,534.57
			23 Jun	Purchases	44,656.42
			28 Jun	Purchases	163.00
30 Jun	Balance c/d	7,258.75			

Bank: £1,661.88 (= £52,345.24 + £7,389.34 + £3,000.00 – £11,532.22 – £769.00 – £52,095.24)

VAT Control: £3,654.90 (= £364.33 + £12,636.87 – £9,346.30)

Discounts allowed: £366.83

Payables ledger control: £7,258.75 (= £14,534.57 + £44,656.42 + £163 – £52,095.24)

(b)

	Debit £	Credit £
Sales		66,035.34
Purchases	42,695.57	
Rent	769.00	
Insurance	2,453.91	
Bank		1,661.88
VAT Control		3,654.90
Payables ledger control		7,258.75
Receivables ledger control	32,325.56	
Discounts allowed	366.83	
Totals	78,610.87	78,610.87

Task 8

	Debit £	Credit £
Sales		71,466.02
Purchases	50,316.01	
Discounts received		993.58
Bank	12,353.56	
Plant and equipment	6,354.47	
Receivables ledger control	3,435.56	
Total	72,459.60	72,459.60

From the list of balances, sales and discounts received are credit balances, while the remaining entries are debit balances. Sales, bank, plant and equipment and the receivables ledger control balances do not require adjustment. Purchases and discounts received do require adjustment as errors have been identified and journals must be processed to correct these entries.

Sales, bank, plant and equipment and receivables ledger control were all balances per the initial trial balances.

Purchases = £45,343.33 (DEBIT) + £4,972.68 (DEBIT) = £50,316.01 (DEBIT).

Discounts received = £964.34 (CREDIT) + £29.24 (CREDIT) = £993.58 (CREDIT).

From this we can deduce that there must have been a suspense account balance of £4,943.44 (CREDIT) (= £4,972.68 (CREDIT) − £29.24 (DEBIT)), which is assumed to have been cleared by the journal.

BPP

BPP Practice Assessment 2

Principles of Bookkeeping Controls

Time allowed: 1 hour and 30 minutes

Principles of Bookkeeping Controls

BPP Practice Assessment 2

Assessment information

You have **1 hour and 30 minutes** to complete this practice assessment.

This assessment contains **8 tasks** and you should attempt to complete **every** task.

Each task is independent. You will not need to refer to your answers to previous tasks.

The total number of marks for this assessment is **80**.

Read every task carefully to make sure you understand what is required.

Where the date is relevant, it is given in the task data.

Both minus signs and brackets can be used to indicate negative numbers **unless** task instructions state otherwise.

You must use a full stop to indicate a decimal point. For example, write 100.57 **not** 100,57 **or** 10057.

You may use a comma to indicate a number in the thousands, but you don't have to. For example, 10000 and 10,000 are both acceptable.

Mathematical rounding should be applied where appropriate.

Task 1 (10 marks)

This task is about using control accounts.

A VAT control account balance is shown in the general ledger.

Required

(a) **Identify which ONE of the following is correct in relation to the VAT control account.**

	✓
A balance brought down on the debit side at the end of the month indicates a VAT liability to HMRC.	
A balance brought down on the credit side at the end of the month indicates a VAT liability to HMRC.	
A payment to HMRC in respect of VAT is recorded on the credit side of the VAT control account.	
Any money received from HMRC in respect of a VAT overpayment is recorded on the debit side of the VAT control account.	

(1 mark)

You work in the accounts department Giovanni Ltd. Your manager has run a report which shows a credit balance on the VAT control account at the end of December of £18,380. The credit balance at the end of November was £14,490. Your manager has asked you to prepare a VAT control account to explain why December shows a higher balance.

The following information has been recorded during the month of December:

	Amount £
VAT on sales	30,240
VAT on purchases	14,320
VAT on sales returns	390
VAT on purchases returns	164
VAT on discounts allowed	540
VAT on discounts received	496
VAT on cash sales	1,040
Payment made to HMRC	12,800

Required

(b) **Complete the VAT control account below for December by selecting account names from the pick list and entering amounts in the spaces provided. You must ensure a number is entered in each space provided.**

VAT Control Account

Details	Amount £	Details	Amount £
		Balance b/d	14,490

Details	Amount £	Details	Amount £
▼		▼	
▼		▼	
▼		▼	
▼		▼	
Balance c/d	18,380		

Picklist

- Bank
- Cash sales
- Discounts allowed
- Discounts received
- Purchases
- Purchases returns
- Sales
- Sales returns

(8 marks)

Carlos Ltd has the following payables ledger control account.

Payables Ledger Control Account

Date	Details	Amount £	Date	Details	Amount £
31/08	Purchases returns	2,185	1/08	Balance b/d	9,487
31/08	Bank	9,204	31/08	Purchases	14,385
31/08	Discounts received	523			
31/08	Balance c/d				

Required

(c) **What will be the balance carried down on the payables ledger control account?**

£ [   ]

(1 mark)

Task 2 (10 marks)

This task is about reconciling control accounts.

The balance on the payables ledger control account will appear in the year-end trial balance. It is important to reconcile this to the payables ledger.

Required

(a) Identify which ONE of the following statements is correct.

	✓
In a digital accounting system, the bookkeeper has to manually total the ledger accounts.	
A trial balance can be automatically created in a manual accounting system.	
In a digital accounting system, sales and purchases invoices are posted to the relevant daybook. From there, the relevant control account and subsidiary ledger are automatically updated.	
In a digital accounting system, once recurring entries are set up, they do not need to be reviewed and updated at regular intervals.	

(1 mark)

These are the accounts in the receivables ledger at 1 October.

Charlotte Ltd

Details	Amount £	Details	Amount £
Balance b/f	8,700		

Anne plc

Details	Amount £	Details	Amount £
Balance b/f	21,500		

Emily & Co

Details	Amount £	Details	Amount £
		Balance b/f	450

Haworths

Details	Amount £	Details	Amount £
Balance b/f	11,200		

Required

(b) (i) What is the total of the balances in the receivables ledger on 1 October?

£ [   ]

(2 marks)

The balance of the receivables ledger control account on 1 October is £41,590.

Required

(ii) What is the difference between the balance of the receivables ledger control account and the total of the balances in the receivables ledger you calculated in (b) (i)?

£ [   ]

(2 marks)

(c) Identify whether or not the reasons below could explain the difference you calculated in (b) (ii).

Reasons	Explains the difference ✓	Does not explain the difference ✓
Goods returned may have been entered in the customer's account in the receivables ledger twice		
Discounts allowed were entered in the receivables ledger control account only		
Goods returned were omitted from the receivables ledger control account		
Goods sold were entered twice in a customer's account in the receivables ledger		
A cheque received was entered in the receivables ledger control account twice		

(5 marks)

Task 3 (8 marks)

This task is about payment methods and reconciling the cash book to the bank statement.

Required

(a) Match each situation with the most appropriate payment method by selecting from the pick list provided.

Situation	Payment method
Making a payment via the internet to purchase office supplies	▼
Making a non-automated low value payment in person	▼
Making a payment to a supplier by post	▼
Making regular payments of set amounts to the same recipient	▼

Picklist
- Cash
- Cheque

 BPP

- Debit card
- Standing order

(4 marks)

(b) Show which TWO of the payment methods below will reduce funds in the payer's bank balance on the date of payment, by ticking the appropriate boxes.

Payment method	Reduce funds on the date of payment ✓
Credit card	
Direct debit	
Cash	
CHAPS	
Cheque	

(2 marks)

(c) Identify whether each of the following statements are true or false.

Statement	True ✓	False ✓
Cheques to suppliers have been prepared and will be posted to suppliers the following day. It is likely that the cash book and bank statement will both be updated on the date the cheques are written in respect of these payments.		
Interest charges incurred in respect of a current account bank overdraft are likely to first appear on the bank statement and then be recorded in the business's cash book.		

(2 marks)

Task 4 (12 marks)

Below is the bank statement for March.

Date 20XX	Details	Paid out £	Paid in £	Balance £
01 Mar	Balance b/f			3,460 C
05 Mar	Cheque 1165	465		2,995 C
12 Mar	Cheque 1167	7,200		4,205 D
15 Mar	GreenBee		9,460	5,255 C
16 Mar	Cheque 1166	533		4,722 C
23 Mar	Port Cookers		7,000	11,722 C
24 Mar	Cheque No 1169	2,400		9,322 C
26 Mar	Bank charges	25		9,297 C

Date 20XX	Details	Paid out £	Paid in £	Balance £
28 Mar	Bank interest		27	9,324 C

D = Debit C = Credit

Cash book

Date 20XX	Details	Bank £	Date 20XX	Cheque number	Details	Bank £
01 Mar	Balance b/f	3,460	02 Mar	1165	Bobbin & Co	465
10 Mar	GreenBee	9,460	03 Mar	1166	Freddies Ltd	533
14 Mar	Port Cookers	7,000	07 Mar	1167	Irons	7,200
21 Mar	Kitchen Co	3,452	05 Mar	1168	Jerry & Co	2,500
23 Mar	Nigella's	2,468	15 Mar	1169	P Smith	2,400
26 Mar	Bank interest	27	23 Mar	1170	J Frost	362
			28 Mar		Bank charges	25

The cash book and bank reconciliation statement for March have not been finalised.

Required

(a) Identify the four transactions that are included in the cash book but are missing from the bank statement and complete the bank reconciliation statement as at 31 March.

Note. Do not make any entries in the shaded boxes.

Bank reconciliation statement		£
Balance per bank statement		9,324
Add:		
	▼	
	▼	
Total to add		
Less:		
	▼	
	▼	
Total to subtract		
Balance as per cash book		12,382

 BPP

Picklist

- Balance b/d
- Balance c/d
- Bank charges
- Bank interest
- Bobbin & Co
- Freddies Ltd
- GreenBee
- Irons
- J Frost
- Jerry & Co
- Kitchen Co
- Nigella's
- P Smith
- Port Cookers

(10 marks)

(b) Refer to the cash book in (a) and check that the bank statement has been correctly reconciled by calculating:

- **The balance carried down**
- **The total of each of the bank columns after the balance carried down has been recorded**

Balance carried down £	Bank column totals £

(2 marks)

Task 5 (10 marks)

This is a customer's account in the receivables ledger.

Bryson Construction

Date 20XX	Details	Amount £	Date 20XX	Details	Amount £
01 Jan	Balance b/f	450	4 Jan	Credit note 45	35
15 Jan	Invoice 951	785	17 Jan	Credit note 46	210

The customer has now ceased trading owing the amount outstanding which includes VAT.

Required

(a) **Record the journal entries needed in the general ledger to write off the net amount and the VAT.**

Account name		Debit £	Credit £
	▼		
	▼		
	▼		

Picklist

- Irrecoverable debt expense
- Receivables ledger control
- VAT control

(6 marks)

A new business has been started and a new set of accounts are to be opened. A partially completed journal to record the opening entries is shown below.

Required

(b) **Complete the journal by ticking either the debit or credit column.**

Account name	Amount £	Debit ✓	Credit ✓
Cash at bank	2,400		
Capital	6,000		
Loan from bank	1,200		
Computer equipment	4,800		

(4 marks)

Task 6 (10 marks)

This task is about using the journal to correct errors.

The journal entries below have been prepared to correct an error.

Journal

Account name	Debit £	Credit £
Heat & Light	1,650	
Suspense		1,650
Suspense	1,560	
Heat & Light		1,560

Required

Post the journal entries in the general ledger accounts below and show the balance carried down in the heat and light account. Show the totals of the debit and credit columns in each account.

Heat & Light

Details	Amount £	Details	Amount £
Balance b/f	4,760	▼	
▼		▼	
Total		Total	

Suspense

Details	Amount £	Details	Amount £
Balance b/f	90	▼	
▼		▼	
Total		Total	

Picklist

- Balance b/f
- Balance c/d
- Heat & Light
- Suspense

(10 marks)

Task 7 (10 marks)

This task is about extracting a trial balance.

Renton runs a shop. Most of the ledger accounts have been closed off and the balances included in the trial balance as at 31 January.

Required

(a) Complete the remaining ledger accounts by inserting the balance carried down on each account. Enter your answers to two decimal places.

VAT control account

Date 20XX	Details	Amount £	Date 20XX	Details	Amount £
31 Jan	Purchases	6,621.48	1 Jan	Balance b/d	3,402.32
31 Jan	Sales returns	451.52	31 Jan	Sales	10,425.00
	Balance c/d		31 Jan	Purchases returns	525.25

Receivables ledger control:

Date 20XX	Details	Amount £	Date 20XX	Details	Amount £
1 Jan	Balance b/d	10,583.91	31 Jan	Sales returns	3,439.53
31 Jan	Sales	30,482.52	31 Jan	Discounts allowed	2,482.62
			31 Jan	Balance c/d	

Discounts received:

Date 20XX	Details	Amount £	Date 20XX	Details	Amount £
31 Jan	Balance c/d		1 Jan	Balance b/d	0.00
			31 Jan	Payables ledger control	1,642.48

Bank loan:

Date 20XX	Details	Amount £	Date 20XX	Details	Amount £
31 Jun	Balance c/d		1 Jan	Balance b/d	8,000.00
			31 Jan	Bank	5,500.00

(4 marks)

(b) Complete the trial balance by inserting the missing figures and calculating the total for each column. Enter your answers to two decimal places.

	Debit £	Credit £
Sales		80,384.62
Purchases	59,325.62	
Advertising	2,425.62	
Bank	16,494.67	
Bank loan		
VAT Control		
Payables ledger control		10,583.52
Receivables ledger control		
Discounts received		
Totals		

(6 marks)

 BPP

Task 8 (10 marks)

This task is about redrafting a trial balance.

On 28 February a trial balance was extracted and did not balance. The debit column totalled £448,100 and the credit column totalled £450,100.

Required

(a) What entry would be made in the suspense account to balance the trial balance? Select whether this would be a debit or a credit.

Account name	Amount	Debit	Credit
	£	✓	✓
Suspense			

(2 marks)

The journal entries to correct all the bookkeeping errors, and a list of balances as they appear in the trial balance, are shown below

Account name	Debit	Credit
	£	£
Suspense	200	
Bank		200
Heat & Light	200	
Bank		200

Account name	Debit	Credit
	£	£
Rent paid	2,500	
Suspense		2,500
Suspense	300	
Advertising		300

Required

(b) Complete the table below to show:

- The balance of each account after the journal entries have been recorded
- Whether each balance will be a debit or credit entry in the trial balance

List of balances

Account name	Original balance	New balance	Debit	Credit
	£	£	✓	✓
Heat & Light	800			

Account name	Original balance	New balance	Debit	Credit
	£	£	✓	✓
Bank (debit)	4,500			
Advertising	960			
Rent paid	6,500			

(8 marks)

BPP Practice Assessment 2

Principles of Bookkeeping Controls

Answers

Task 1

(a) The correct answer is:

	✓
A balance brought down on the debit side at the end of the month indicates a VAT liability to HMRC.	
A balance brought down on the credit side at the end of the month indicates a VAT liability to HMRC.	✓
A payment to HMRC in respect of VAT is recorded on the credit side of the VAT control account.	
Any money received from HMRC in respect of a VAT overpayment is recorded on the debit side of the VAT control account.	

A balance brought down on the credit side at the end of the month indicates a VAT liability to HMRC.

In relation to statement of financial position items, balances brought down on the credit side of ledger accounts represent liabilities. Therefore, a balance brought down on the debit side at the end of the month would be an asset (in this case, an amount due from HMRC to the business).

A payment to HMRC in respect of VAT is recorded on the credit side of the cash book and the debit side of the VAT control account, being a reduction in the liability.

Any money received from HMRC is recorded on the credit side of the VAT control account and the debit side of the cash book. This reduces the amount the business owes HMRC in future periods and therefore is a reduction in the VAT liability.

(b)

VAT Control Account

Details	Amount £	Details	Amount £
		Balance b/d	14,490
Purchases	14,320	Sales	30,240
Sales returns	390	Purchases returns	164
Discounts allowed	540	Discounts received	496
Bank	12,800	Cash sales	1,040
Balance c/d	18,380		

(c) £ 11,960

= Total of credit entries − total of debit entries

= (£9,487 + £14,385) − (£2,185 + £9,204 + £523)

BPP

Task 2

(a) The correct answer is:

	✓
In a digital accounting system, the bookkeeper has to manually total the ledger accounts.	
A trial balance can be automatically created in a manual accounting system.	
In a digital accounting system, sales and purchases invoices are posted to the relevant daybook. From there, the relevant control account and subsidiary ledger are automatically updated.	✓
In a digital accounting system, once recurring entries are set up, they do not need to be reviewed and updated at regular intervals.	

In a digital accounting system, sales and purchases invoices are posted to the relevant daybook. From there, the relevant control account and subsidiary ledger are automatically updated.

This is one of the benefits of a digital accounting system; it is efficient and reduces the risk of errors occurring in the accounting records as there are fewer manual processes.

In respect of the other statements:

A digital accounting system will total the ledger accounts; this is not a task the bookkeeper is required to perform.

A trial balance can be automatically created in a digital accounting system but not in a manual accounting system.

Where recurring entries are set up in a digital accounting system, they must be reviewed and updated where necessary. The amount that must be paid or the due date will change periodically and therefore such entries must be agreed to supplier documentation on a regular basis.

(b) (i) £ 40,950

Working

£8,700 + £21,500 − £450 + £11,200 = £40,950

(ii) £ 640

Working

£41,590 − £40,950 = £640

(c) The correct answers are:

Reasons	Explains the difference ✓	Does not explain the difference ✓
Goods returned may have been entered in the customer's account in the receivables ledger twice	✓	
Discounts allowed were entered in the receivables ledger control account only		✓

Reasons	Explains the difference ✓	Does not explain the difference ✓
Goods returned were omitted from the receivables ledger control account	✓	
Goods sold were entered twice in a customer's account in the receivables ledger		✓
A cheque received was entered in the receivables ledger control account twice		✓

Task 3

(a)

Situation	Payment method
Making a payment via the internet to purchase office supplies	Debit card
Making a non-automated low value payment in person	Cash
Making a payment to a supplier by post	Cheque
Making regular payments of set amounts to the same recipient	Standing order

(b)

Payment method	Reduce funds on the date of payment ✓
Credit card	
Direct debit	✓
Cash	
CHAPS	✓
Cheque	

(c) The correct answers are:

Statement	True ✓	False ✓
Cheques to suppliers have been prepared and will be posted to suppliers the following day. It is likely that the cash book and bank statement will both be updated on the date the cheques are written in respect of these payments.		✓
Interest charges incurred in respect of a current account bank overdraft are likely to first appear on the bank statement and then be recorded in the business's cash book.	✓	

The cheques that are ready to be posted to suppliers will have been entered in the cash book. However, the suppliers have not yet received them or paid them into their respective bank accounts, therefore, they will not yet have cleared the business's bank statement.

Task 4

(a)

Bank reconciliation statement	£
Balance per bank statement	9,324
Add:	
Nigella's	2,468
Kitchen Co	3,452
Total to add	5,920
Less:	
Jerry & Co	2,500
J Frost	362
Total to subtract	2,862
Balance as per cash book	12,382

(b)

Balance carried down £	Bank column totals £
12,382	25,867

Working

Cash book

Date 20XX	Details	Bank £	Date 20XX	Cheque number	Details	Bank £
01 Mar	Balance b/f	3,460	02 Mar	1165	Bobbin & Co	465
10 Mar	GreenBee	9,460	03 Mar	1166	Freddies Ltd	533
14 Mar	Port Cookers	7,000	07 Mar	1167	Irons	7,200
21 Mar	Kitchen Co	3,452	05 Mar	1168	Jerry & Co	2,500
23 Mar	Nigella's	2,468	15 Mar	1169	P Smith	2,400
26 Mar	Bank interest	27	23 Mar	1170	J Frost	362
			28 Mar		Bank charges	25
			31 Mar		Balance c/d	12,382
		25,867				25,867

 BPP

Date 20XX	Details	Bank £	Date 20XX	Cheque number	Details	Bank £
1 Apr	Balance b/d	12,382				

Task 5

(a)

Account name	Debit £	Credit £
Irrecoverable debt expense	825	
Receivables ledger control		990
VAT control	165	

(b)

Account name	Amount £	Debit ✓	Credit ✓
Cash at bank	2,400	✓	
Capital	6,000		✓
Loan from bank	1,200		✓
Computer equipment	4,800	✓	

Task 6

Heat & Light

Details	Amount £	Details	Amount £
Balance b/f	4,760	Suspense	1,560
Suspense	1,650	Balance c/d	4,850
Total	6,410	Total	6,410

Suspense

Details	Amount £	Details	Amount £
Balance b/f	90	Heat & Light	1,650
Heat & Light	1,560	Balance c/d	
Total	1,650	Total	1,650

BPP

ANSWERS

Task 7

(a)

VAT control account

Date 20XX	Details	Amount £	Date 20XX	Details	Amount £
31 Jan	Purchases	6,621.48	1 Jan	Balance b/d	3,402.32
31 Jan	Sales returns	451.52	31 Jan	Sales	10,425.00
	Balance c/d	7,279.57	31 Jan	Purchases returns	525.25

Receivables ledger control:

Date 20XX	Details	Amount £	Date 20XX	Details	Amount £
1 Jan	Balance b/d	10,583.91	31 Jan	Sales returns	3,439.53
31 Jan	Sales	30,482.52	31 Jan	Discounts allowed	2,482.62
			31 Jan	Balance c/d	35,144.28

Discounts received:

Date 20XX	Details	Amount £	Date 20XX	Details	Amount £
31 Jan	Balance c/d	1,642.48	1 Jan	Balance b/d	0.00
			31 Jan	Payables ledger control	1,642.48

Bank loan:

Date 20XX	Details	Amount £	Date 20XX	Details	Amount £
31 Jun	Balance c/d	13,500.00	1 Jan	Balance b/d	8,000.00
			31 Jan	Bank	5,500.00

(b)

	Debit £	Credit £
Sales		80,384.62
Purchases	59,325.62	
Advertising	2,425.62	
Bank	16,494.67	
Bank loan		13,500.00
VAT Control		7,279.57
Payables ledger control		10,583.52
Receivables ledger control	35,144.28	
Discounts received		1,642.48
Totals	113,390.19	113,390.19

Task 8

(a)

Account name	Amount £	Debit ✓	Credit ✓
Suspense	2,000	✓	

(b)

List of balances

Account name	Original balance £	New balance £	Debit ✓	Credit ✓
Heat & Light	800	1,000	✓	
Bank (debit)	4,500	4,100	✓	
Advertising	960	660	✓	
Rent paid	6,500	9,000	✓	

Working

Heat & Light	£800 + £200 = £1,000
Bank (debit)	£4,500 – £200 – £200 = £4,100
Advertising	£960 – £300 = £660
Rent paid	£6,500 + £2,500 = £9,000

 BPP

BPP Practice Assessment 3

Principles of Bookkeeping Controls

Time allowed: 1 hour 30 minutes

Principles of Bookkeeping Controls

BPP Practice Assessment 3

Assessment information

You have **1 hour** and **30 minutes** to complete this practice assessment.

This assessment contains **8 tasks** and you should attempt to complete every task.

Each task is independent. You will not need to refer to your answers to previous tasks.

The total number of marks for this assessment is **80**.

Read every task carefully to make sure you understand what is required.

Where the date is relevant, it is given in the task data.

Both minus signs and brackets can be used to indicate negative numbers **unless** task instructions state otherwise.

You must use a full stop to indicate a decimal point. For example, write 100.57 **not** 100,57 or 10057.

You may use a comma to indicate a number in the thousands, but you don't have to. For example, 10000 and 10,000 are both acceptable.

Mathematical rounding should be applied where appropriate.

Task 1 (10 marks)

This task is about using control accounts.

Required

(a) **Identify whether the following statements are true or false.**

Statement	True ✓	False ✓
A debit balance on the receivables control account means that an error has been made in posting entries to the general ledger.		
A receivables ledger control account allows a business to identify the amount owed by individual customers at a point in time.		

(2 marks)

You have printed a report which shows the total amount owed to suppliers is £37,008 at the end of March. Your manager is surprised that so much is owed as only £5,600 was owed at the end of February. He has asked you to prepare a payables ledger control account.

You have identified the following information:

Details-March	Total amount £	VAT £	Net amount £
Purchases daybook	38,400	6,400	32,000
Purchases returns daybook	2,880	480	2,400
Discounts received daybook	912	152	760
Cash book – payments to suppliers	3,200		

Required

(b) **Complete the table below to show the entries in the payables ledger control account. Ensure numbers are included in either the debit or credit column. You do not need to type anything in unused spaces.**

Payables ledger control account	Debit £	Credit £
1 March Balance b/d		
Purchases daybook		
Purchases returns daybook		
Discounts received daybook		
Cash book – payments to suppliers		
31 March Balance c/d		

(6 marks)

You have printed a report which shows the balance brought down on the VAT control account at 1 May is a credit balance of £1,129.

The following information is available for April:

Details – April	Total amount £
VAT on sales	9,870
VAT on purchases	2,826
Bank payment to HMRC	18,380

There have been no sale or purchase returns during April and no discounts have been given to customers or received from suppliers.

Required

(c) Calculate the balance on the VAT control account on 1 April.

£ [   ] [▼]

Picklist

- Credit
- Debit

(2 marks)

Task 2 (10 marks)

This task is about reconciling control accounts.

Required

(a) Complete the following statements by selecting an option from each picklist below.

Reconciling the payables ledger control account to the receivables ledger may identify errors

in [(1)   ▼] .

An error in the payables ledger [(2)   ▼] affect the trial balance.

Picklist 1

- Both the payables ledger control account and the payables ledger
- The payables ledger control account only
- The payables ledger only

Picklist 2

- Will
- Will not

(2 marks)

You work in the accounts department of a stationery manufacturer. The following customer accounts make up the receivables ledger at 1 April.

Pure Pencils Company:

Details	Amount £	Details	Amount £
Balance b/d	64,474		

Details	Amount £	Details	Amount £

Pens and Stuff:

Details	Amount £	Details	Amount £
Balance b/d	32,575		

Pence Pens Ltd:

Details	Amount £	Details	Amount £
Balance b/d	2,463		

Art Supplies Ltd:

Details	Amount £	Details	Amount £
		Balance b/d	12,529

Required

(b) (i) What is the balance on the receivables ledger at 1 April?

£ ⬚ **(1 mark)**

The balance on the receivables ledger control account on 1 April is a debit balance of £88,279.

Required

(ii) What is the difference between the balance on the receivables ledger and the receivables ledger control account?

£ ⬚ **(1 mark)**

(c) Identify whether the following statements are true or false.

Statement	True ✓	False ✓
A purchase of £300 was posted to the wrong side of the individual supplier account. This will result in a difference between the payables ledger and the payables ledger control account of £300.		

Statement	True ✓	False ✓
A cash receipt from a credit customer of £1,400 was recorded in the receivables ledger control account but was missed from the individual customer account. The receivables ledger control account will show a balance of £1,400 less than the total in the receivables ledger.		
A discount allowed of £100 was recorded as a sales return of £100 in the individual accounts. This will result in a difference between the receivables ledger and the receivables ledger control account of £200.		
A purchase return of £150 has been recorded twice in the individual customer account but correctly in the control account. The balance of the payables ledger control account will be £150 higher than the payables ledger balance.		
HMRC is included as a customer when preparing the receivables ledger control account.		
A discount allowed of £250 was posted twice to the individual customer account but only recorded once in the receivables ledger control account. This will result in the balance on the receivables ledger control account being £250 less than the receivables ledger balance.		

(6 marks)

Task 3 (8 marks)

This task is about payment methods and reconciling the cash book to the bank statement.

Required

(a) **Identify whether the following payment methods impact the bank immediately (same day) or at a later date.**

Payment method	Immediate ✓	Later date ✓
Credit card		
Standing order		

(2 marks)

There are many transactions that can result in a difference between the bank statement and the cash book.

Required

(b) **Select ONE reason for a difference between the bank statement and the cash book that matches each description using the pick list provided.**

Description	Option
The accounts clerk realised that a large amount of money from cash sales had accumulated and decided to take this to the bank.	▼

Description	Option
Cheques received from customers were paid into the bank just before the month end but do not appear on the bank statement.	▼
The telephone bill for the month was automatically paid out of the bank account.	▼
The business has paid suppliers by cheque totalling £1,560 during the month. These amounts do not appear on the bank statement.	▼

Picklist

- Bank charges
- Counter credit
- Direct debit
- Outstanding lodgements
- Unpresented cheques

(4 marks)

(c) **Identify if the following adjustments will need to be made in the cash book, the bank reconciliation, both, or neither.**

Description	Cash book ✓	Bank reconciliation ✓	Both ✓	Neither ✓
A credit purchase was recorded as a cash purchase. The supplier had not been paid by the period end.				
A supplier who was owed £1,800 was only paid £1,520 when taking advantage of a prompt payment discount.				

(2 marks)

Task 4 (12 marks)

This task is about reconciling a bank statement with the cash book.

You have been provided with the cash book and bank statement for September for Kids R Uz Co, a business selling children's toys.

Cash book

Date 20XX	Details	£	Date 20XX	Details	£
2 Sep	Elsa Hernandez	2,899	1 Sep	Bal b/d	6,489
4 Sep	Alberto Arwan	3,299	3 Sep	All Toys Co	1,600

 BPP

Date 20XX	Details	£	Date 20XX	Details	£
5 Sep	Thiago De Souza	2,799	19 Sep	The Toy Centre	2,230
17 Sep	Hector Chen	2,399	28 Sep	The Plastic Box	1,786
28 Sep	Felix Garcia	1,899		Bal c/d	1,190

The bank statement for the same period is as follows:

Date 20XX	Details	Paid in £	Paid out £	Balance £
1 Sep	Opening balance			3,438 D
5 Sep	Transfer – Thiago De Souza	2,799		639 D
8 Sep	Elsa Hernandez – cheque	2,899		2,260 C
8 Sep	Alberto Arwan – cheque	3,299		5,559 C
12 Sep	Cheque 00643		3,051	2,508 C
15 Sep	Counter – credit	1,500		4,008 C
18 Sep	Direct Debit – Broadband Co		285	3,723 C
18 Sep	Cheque – Hector Chen	2,399		6,122 C
20 Sep	Cheque 00645		2,230	3,892 C
30 Sep	Cheque 00646		1,786	2,106 C

Required

Update the cash book and prepare a bank reconciliation at 30 September.

Cash book		Debit £	Credit £
Closing balance b/d			
Adjustments:			
(1)	▼		
(1)	▼		
Adjusted closing balance			

Picklist 1

- Alberto Arwan – cheque
- Cheque 00643
- Cheque – 00645
- Cheque – 00646
- Cheque – Hector Chen
- Counter – credit
- Direct Debit – Broadband Co

- Elsa Hernandez – cheque
- Transfer – Thiago De Souza

Bank reconciliation	£
Closing balance per bank statement	
Add:	
(2) ▼	
Less:	
(2) ▼	
Adjusted balance	

Picklist 2

- Alberto Arwan
- All Toys Co
- Elsa Hernandez
- Felix Garcia
- Hector Chen
- The Plastic Box
- The Toy Centre
- Thiago De Souza

(12 marks)

Task 5 (10 marks)

This task is about using the journal.

Marek runs a small fast food business. He has produced accounts using a spreadsheet up until 1 January 20X0 but now wishes to start using a cloud accounting system.

The following items need to be included as opening balances in the new accounting system:

Kebab van (asset)	£8,000
Ingredients (inventory)	£80
Bank overdraft	£110
Capital	£7,970

Required

(a) Complete the journal below by entering the opening balance in either the debit or credit column for each item. You do not need to enter anything in the unused columns.

Date	Description	Debit £	Credit £
1/1/X0	Capital		
1/1/X0	Assets		
1/1/X0	Bank		
1/1/X0	Inventory		

(4 marks)

Remy runs a small accounting practice. He has recorded the following year-end journal in his accounting system:

Date of journal: 31 December				Journal number: 008
Date	Description	Debit £	Credit £	
31 Dec	Receivables ledger control		749	Write off an irrecoverable debt
31 Dec	Irrecoverable debts expense	749		Write off an irrecoverable debt

The receivables ledger control account has a closing balance before processing this journal of £2,593 (DR).

Required

(b) After the journal is processed, what will be the revised balance carried down on the receivables ledger control account?

£ [   ]   (1 mark)

Antonio employs 2 people in his business. At 31 March, he needs to prepare a journal to reflect the following information:

- Gross pay to employees – £18,385
- Income tax deducted from gross pay – £2,658
- National insurance contributions deducted from gross pay – £2,601
- Employer's national insurance contributions – £2,147

Required

(c) Complete the journal entries below by entering the correct amount in either the debit or credit column for each line.

Date	Description	Debit £	Credit £
31 March	7000 – Gross wages		
31 March	7006 – Employer NI		
31 March	2210 – PAYE		
31 March	2211 – National Insurance		
31 March	2220 – Net wages		

(5 marks)

Task 6 (10 marks)

This task is about using the journal to correct errors.

Required

(a) Identify the type of error described by each of the following statements by dragging the appropriate option into the space provided.

	Type of error
Hafiz bought some office stationery but coded the expense to rent instead of stationery.	▼
Thibault quoted a customer £800 but invoiced £8,000.	▼
Seema entered a payment to a credit customer as £250 instead of £520.	▼
Mary coded an invoice for her petrol expenses to motor vehicle purchases.	▼

Picklist

- Compensating errors
- Error of commission
- Error of omission
- Error of original entry
- Error of principle
- Reversal of entries

(4 marks)

A payment was received into the bank account of £606. This was from a credit customer who owed £660 but the bank transfer had been mis-typed. As the system could not identify an invoice to allocate the receipt to, it allocated it to the suspense account. This was the only entry in the suspense account as at 30 June.

Required

(b) Identify the balance on the suspense account in the trial balance by entering an amount in the debit or credit column below.

Account	Debit £	Credit £
Suspense		

(1 marks)

The following errors have been identified when reviewing the year end accounts of Vantastic Ltd.

- A single payment to a supplier of £990 related to two separate invoices of £660 and £330. As the system was unable to match the payment to a supplier invoice, it was included in the suspense account.

- A telephone expense of £270 has been coded to the rent expense account.

Required

(c) Show the journal entries required to correct these errors by entering the correct amount in either the debit or credit column for each account.

Date of journal: 30 June				Journal number: 242
Date	Description	Debit £		Credit £
30 June	Telephone expense			
30 June	Rent expense			
30 June	Suspense			
30 June	Payables ledger control account			

(4 marks)

Sarah runs a very small business selling picture frames. As she only has a few transactions each month, she has chosen to operate a manual accounting system. She paid a supplier £36 directly into their bank account and she recorded this as:

Credit Bank £36

Credit Payables ledger control account £36.

She also debited the individual account in the payables ledger.

Required

(d) **Complete the following statement.**

The amount that will be included in the suspense account is [▼]

Picklist

- £36 Credit
- £36 Debit
- £72 Credit
- £72 Debit

(1 mark)

Task 7 (10 marks)

This task is about extracting a trial balance.

Liv has a garden supplies business. Most of the ledger accounts have been closed off and included in the trial balance as at 31 January.

Required

(a) **Complete the remaining ledger accounts by inserting the balance carried down on each account. Enter all answers to two decimal places.**

Plant and equipment:

Date 20XX	Details	Amount £	Date 20XX	Details	Amount £
1 Jan	Balance b/d	15,000.00			
27 Jan	Bank	82,500.00			
			31 Jan	Balance c/d	

 BPP

Sales returns:

Date 20XX	Details	Amount £	Date 20XX	Details	Amount £
1 Jan	Balance b/d	0.00			
21 Jan	Receivables ledger control account	7,236.00			
			31 Jan	Balance c/d	

Capital:

Date 20XX	Details	Amount £	Date 20XX	Details	Amount £
13 Jan	Bank	51,000.00	1 Jan	Balance b/d	165,000.00
31 Jan	Balance c/d				

Receivables ledger control account:

Date 20XX	Details	Amount £	Date 20XX	Details	Amount £
1 Jan	Balance b/d	96,558.00	20 Jan	Sales returns	7,236.00
31 Jan	Sales	131,307.09	29 Jan	Irrecoverable debt	18,072.00
			30 Jan	Bank	141,001.99
			31 Jan	Balance c/d	

(4 marks)

(b) Complete the trial balance by inserting the missing figures and calculating the total for each column. Enter your answers to two decimal places.

	Debit £	Credit £
Sales		131,307.09
Purchases	97,361.67	
Irrecoverable debts	18,072.00	
Bank	7,856.94	
Plant and equipment		
Capital		
Payables ledger control		44,274.62

 BPP

	Debit £	Credit £
Receivables ledger control		
Sales returns		
Totals		

(6 marks)

Task 8 (10 marks)

This task is about redrafting a trial balance.

The initial list of balances for Olga's business at 31 December is:

Item	£
Sales	313,248.15
Wages	232,023.33
Irrecoverable debts	4,010.55
Rent	23,720.80
Cash	8,117.17
Drawings	47,500.00

Some year-end errors have been identified and the following journals are required to be processed:

Date of journal: 31 December				Journal number: 066	
Date	Description	Debit	Credit	Description	
31 December	Irrecoverable debts	1,067.50		Irrecoverable debt not initially coded.	
31 December	Suspense		1,067.50	Irrecoverable debt not initially coded.	
31 December	Suspense	3,191.20		Rent refund not coded.	
31 December	Rent		3,191.20	Rent refund not coded.	

Required

Complete the adjusted trial balance by inserting the correct figures in either the debit or credit column and entering totals for each column.

	Debit £	Credit £
Sales		
Wages		
Irrecoverable debts		
Rent		

 BPP

	Debit £	Credit £
Cash		
Drawings		
Total		

(10 marks)

BPP Practice Assessment 3

Principles of Bookkeeping Controls

Answers

Task 1

(a) The correct answers are:

Statement	True ✓	False ✓
A debit balance on the receivables control account means that an error has been made in posting entries to the general ledger.		✓
A receivables ledger control account allows a business to identify the amount owed by individual customers at a point in time.		✓

A debit balance on the receivables ledger control account is to be expected as amounts owed by credit customers are an asset of the business and therefore a debit item. This does not mean that an error has been made.

It is incorrect to state that a receivables ledger control account allows a business to identify the amounts owed by individual customers. This is the function of the receivables ledger; the control account merely contains totals posted from the books of original entry, and does not feature details of any individual customers. The receivables ledger control account shows the total amount owed to the business from all of its customers.

(b)

Payables ledger control account	Debit £	Credit £
1 March Balance b/d		5,600
Purchases daybook		38,400
Purchases returns daybook	2,880	
Discounts received daybook	912	
Cash book – payments to suppliers	3,200	
31 March Balance c/d	37,008	

To calculate the balance carried down, first total the debit and credit columns to identify the higher of the two sides. Here the credit column casts to £44,000 whereas the debit column casts to £6,992. The difference between the totals of £37,008 is the balance carried down. As the total of the debit side is the lower of the two columns, the balance carried down is shown on the debit side of the payables ledger control account so that the debit and credit columns balance.

(c) £ | 12,465 | | Credit |

This can be calculated using a T-account, as follows:

VAT Control:

Date 20XX	Details	Amount £	Date 20XX	Details	Amount £
April	Purchases	2,826	1 April	Balance b/d (missing figure)	12,465

 BPP

Date 20XX	Details	Amount £	Date 20XX	Details	Amount £
April	Bank payment to HMRC	18,380	April	Sales	9,870
1 May	Balance c/d	1,129			
	Total	22,335		Total	22,335

The balance b/d is calculated as:

= Total of debit entries – total of credit entries

= (£2,826 + £18,380 + £1,129) – (£9,870)

Task 2

(a) Reconciling the payables ledger control account to the receivables ledger may identify errors

in | both the payables ledger control account and the payables ledger | .

An error in the payables ledger | will not | affect the trial balance.

An error that affects either of the payables ledger control account or the payables ledger will result in a difference between the two. This difference would be found by reconciling them with each other.

Since the payables ledger is a memorandum account only, an error therein will not affect the nominal ledger or the trial balance.

(b) (i) £ | 86,983 |

= £64,474 + £32,575 + £2,463 – £12,529

(ii) £ | 1,296 |

= £88,279 – £86,983

(c) The correct answers are:

Statement	True ✓	False ✓
A purchase of £300 was posted to the wrong side of the individual supplier account. This will result in a difference between the payables ledger and the payables ledger control account of £300.		✓
A cash receipt from a credit customer of £1,400 was recorded in the receivables ledger control account but was missed from the individual customer account. The receivables ledger control account will show a balance of £1,400 less than the total in the receivables ledger.	✓	
A discount allowed of £100 was recorded as a sales return of £100 in the individual accounts. This will result in a difference between the receivables ledger and the receivables ledger control account of £200.		✓

Statement	True ✓	False ✓
A purchase return of £150 has been recorded twice in the individual customer account but correctly in the control account. The balance of the payables ledger control account will be £150 higher than the payables ledger balance.	✓	
HMRC is included as a customer when preparing the receivables ledger control account.		✓
A discount allowed of £250 was posted twice to the individual customer account but only recorded once in the receivables ledger control account. This will result in the balance on the receivables ledger control account being £250 less than the receivables ledger balance.		✓

Task 3

(a) The correct answers are:

Payment method	Immediate ✓	Later date ✓
Credit card		✓
Standing order	✓	

A credit card allows a payment to be made immediately to a supplier, but on credit from the credit card company, which does not then need to be paid immediately by the company itself.

A standing order is a form of regular bank transfer, which would affect the bank statement as soon as it is paid out.

(b)

Description	Option
The accounts clerk realised that a large amount of money from cash sales had accumulated and decided to take this to the bank.	Counter credit
Cheques received from customers were paid into the bank just before the month end but do not appear on the bank statement.	Outstanding lodgements
The telephone bill for the month was automatically paid out of the bank account.	Direct debit
The business has paid suppliers by cheque totalling £1,560 during the month. These amounts do not appear on the bank statement.	Unpresented cheques

ANSWERS

(c) The correct answers are:

Description	Cash book ✓	Bank reconciliation ✓	Both ✓	Neither ✓
A credit purchase was recorded as a cash purchase. The supplier had not been paid by the period end.	✓			
A supplier who was owed £1,800 was only paid £1,520 when taking advantage of a prompt payment discount.				✓

If a credit purchase was recorded as a cash purchase then the cash book will mistakenly show a cash payment which was not in fact made, and will therefore need to be adjusted.

If a supplier was paid an amount after deducting a discount then this would not affect the cash book or the bank reconciliation, since these records merely record payments and receipts. There would, however, be an impact on the payables ledger and the payables ledger control account if the discount were not also recorded there.

Task 4

Cash book	Debit £	Credit £
Closing balance b/d	1,190	
Adjustments:		
Counter – credit	1,500	
Direct Debit – Broadband Co		285
Adjusted closing balance	2,405	

Bank reconciliation	£
Closing balance per bank statement	2,106
Add:	
Felix Garcia	1,899
Less:	
All Toys Co	1,600
Adjusted balance	2,405

Task 5

(a)

Date	Description	Debit £	Credit £
1/1/X0	Capital		7,970
1/1/X0	Assets	8,000	
1/1/X0	Bank		110
1/1/X0	Inventory	80	

(b) £ 1,844

= £2,593 – £749

(c)

Date	Description	Debit £	Credit £
31 March	7000 – Gross wages	18,385	
31 March	7006 – Employer NI	2,147	
31 March	2210 – PAYE		2,658
31 March	2211 – National Insurance (£2,601 + £2,147)		4,748
31 March	2220 – Net wages (balancing figure)		13,126

Task 6

(a)

	Type of error
Hafiz bought some office stationery but coded the expense to rent instead of stationery.	Error of commission
Thibault quoted a customer £800 but invoiced £8,000.	Error of original entry
Seema entered a payment to a credit customer as £250 instead of £520.	Error of original entry
Mary coded an invoice for her petrol expenses to motor vehicle purchases.	Error of principle

The first error is an error of commission because the wrong account has been used, but this does not affect the statement of financial position in relation to the statement of profit or loss.

The second error is an error of original entry because the entries balance but are merely for the wrong amount. The same is the case for the third error.

The final error is an error of principle, because the wrong account has been used and this does affect the statement of financial position vis-a-vis the statement of profit or loss.

 BPP

(b)

Account	Debit £	Credit £
Suspense		606

The customer has paid the wrong amount – £606 instead of £660 – which meant that the system could not match this up with the related invoice. As a result the £606 was put into a suspense account, as an unallocated receipt. The original £660 would still be held within the receivables ledger control account (and also the customer's account in the receivable ledger), but this does not affect the suspense account.

(c)

Date of journal: 30 June			Journal number: 242
Date	Description	Debit £	Credit £
30 June	Telephone expense	270	
30 June	Rent expense		270
30 June	Suspense		990
30 June	Payables ledger control account	990	

The two invoices that were paid together as £990 need to be moved from the suspense account into the payables ledger control account. The original entry would have been to Debit Suspense £990 / Credit Bank £990, which creates a debit of £990 in the suspense account. This is cleared by Credit Suspense and Debit Payables ledger control account.

The miscoding of the telephone expense to rent would not result in a suspense balance as such, and merely needs to be moved from the rent account to the telephone expense account.

(d) The amount that will be included in the suspense account is $\boxed{\text{£72 Debit}}$

The original entry was:

Credit Bank	£36
Credit Payables ledger control account	£36

The transaction should have been recorded as:

Credit Bank	£36
Debit Payables ledger control account	£36

Therefore instead of a debit of £36 Sarah has posted an additional credit of £36. There will therefore be an excess £72 credit balance in the nominal ledger and trial balance, meaning that a suspense balance of £72 debit will be required to make the trial balance balance correctly.

Task 7

(a)

Plant and equipment:

Date 20XX	Details	Amount £	Date 20XX	Details	Amount £
1 Jan	Balance b/d	15,000.00			
27 Jan	Bank	82,500.00			
			31 Jan	Balance c/d	97,500.00

Sales returns:

Date 20XX	Details	Amount £	Date 20XX	Details	Amount £
1 Jan	Balance b/d	0.00			
21 Jan	Receivables ledger control account	7,236.00			
			31 Jan	Balance c/d	7,236.00

Capital:

Date 20XX	Details	Amount £	Date 20XX	Details	Amount £
13 Jan	Bank	51,000.00	1 Jan	Balance b/d	165,000.00
31 Jan	Balance c/d	114,000.00			

Receivables ledger control account:

Date 20XX	Details	Amount £	Date 20XX	Details	Amount £
1 Jan	Balance b/d	96,558.00	20 Jan	Sales returns	7,236.00
31 Jan	Sales	131,307.09	29 Jan	Irrecoverable debt	18,072.00
			30 Jan	Bank	141,001.99
			31 Jan	Balance c/d	61,555.10

The balance for each account is calculated as the difference between the totals of each column.

(b)

	Debit £	Credit £
Sales		131,307.09
Purchases	97,361.67	
Irrecoverable debts	18,072.00	
Bank	7,856.94	
Plant and equipment	97,500.00	
Capital		114,000.00
Payables ledger control		44,274.62
Receivables ledger control	61,555.10	
Sales returns	7,236.00	
Totals	289,581.71	289,581.71

The trial balance is completed by inserting the figures from the accounts that were balanced in part (a), and then calculating the total for each column.

Task 8

	Debit £	Credit £
Sales		313,248.15
Wages	232,023.33	
Irrecoverable debts	5,078.05	
Rent	20,529.60	
Cash	8,117.17	
Drawings	47,500.00	
Total	313,248.15	313,248.15

From the list of balances, Sales is a credit balance, while the remaining entries are debit balances. Sales, wages, cash and the drawings balance do not require adjustment. Irrecoverable debts and rent do require adjustment as errors have been identified and journals must be processed to correct these entries.

(1) Balances per the initial trial balances.

(2) Irrecoverable debts = £4,010.55 (Debit) + £1,067.50 (Debit) = £5,078.05 (Debit).

(3) Rent = £23,720.80 (Debit) – £3,191.20 (Credit) = £20,529.60 (Debit).

From this we can deduce that there must have been a suspense account balance of £2,123.70 (Credit) (= £3,191.20 (Credit) – £1,067.50 (Debit)), which is assumed to have been cleared by the journal.

Tell us what you think

Got comments or feedback on this book? Let us know.
Use your QR code reader:

Or, visit:
https://www.smartsurvey.co.uk/s/GPUBYI/

Need to get in touch with customer service?

www.bpp.com/request-support

Spotted an error?

https://learningmedia.bpp.com/pages/errata